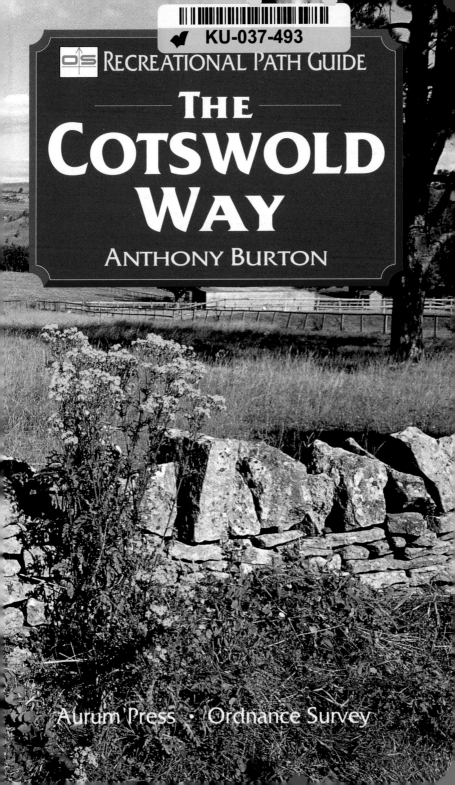

KU-037-493

RECREATIONAL PATH GUIDE

THE COTSWOLD WAY

ANTHONY BURTON

Aurum Press · Ordnance Survey

Acknowledgements

Unless otherwise stated, all photographs in this book are reproduced by kind permission of Gloucestershire County Council (photographer: Steve Dorey). Other photographs are reproduced by kind permission of the following: Stroud District Council: pp. 88, 98-9, 105; John Blake Picture Library: pp. 18, 23; Unichrome (Bath) Ltd: pp. 28, 134-5; Bath City Council: pp. 126-7.

Stroud District Council publishes a series of circular walks based on the Cotswold Way.

Title page: Leckhampton Hill from the Vale of Gloucester
Front cover: Cam Long Down from Uley Bury (Gloucestershire County Council)

First published 1995 by Aurum Press Limited,
25 Bedford Avenue, London WC1B 3AT,
in association with the Ordnance Survey.

Text copyright © Anthony Burton 1995
Maps Crown copyright © Ordnance Survey 1995

A catalogue record for this book is available from the British Library.

ISBN 1 85410 317 2

Book design by Robert Updegraff
Printed and bound in Italy by Printers Srl Trento

CONTENTS

How to use this guide

This guide is in three parts:

- The introduction, historical background to the area and advice for walkers.
- The path itself, described in seven chapters, with maps opposite each route description. This part of the guide also includes information on places of interest as well as a number of related short circular walks. Key sites are numbered in the text and on the maps to make it easy to follow the route description.
- The last part includes useful information such as local transport, accommodation, organisations involved with the path, and further reading.

The maps have been prepared by the Ordnance Survey for this guide using 1:25 000 Pathfinder maps as a base. The line of the Cotswold Way is shown in yellow, with the status of each section of the path – footpath or bridleway for example – shown in green underneath (see key on inside front cover). These rights of way markings also indicate the precise alignment of the path at the time of the original surveys, but in some cases the yellow line on these maps may show a route which is different from that shown by those older surveys, and in such cases walkers are recommended to follow the yellow route in this guide. Any parts of the path that may be difficult to follow on the ground are clearly highlighted in the route description, and important points to watch for are marked with letters in each chapter, both in the text and on the maps. *Some maps start on a right-hand page and continue on the left-hand page – black arrows (→) at the edge of the maps indicate the start point.* Should there have been a need to alter the route since publication of this guide for any reason, walkers are advised to follow the waymarks or signs which have been put up on site to indicate this.

DISTANCE CHECKLIST

This list will help you in calculating the distances between places on the Cotswold Way, whether you are planning your overnight stays, or checking your progress.

Location	Approximate distance from previous location	
	miles	km
Chipping Campden Market Hall	0	0
Broadway	5.0	8
Stanway	5.9	9.5
Hailes Abbey	4.0	6.5
Winchcombe	1.9	3
Belas Knap	2.5	4
Cleeve Hill	4.0	6.5
Reservoir Inn (A40)	5.0	8
Seven Springs crossroads (by alternative route)	3.7	6
Leckhampton Hill	1.9	3
Crickley Hill	3.1	5
Cooper's Hill	4.7	7.5
Painswick	4.0	6.5
Haresfield Beacon	2.8	4.5
Stanley Mill	4.3	7
Uley Bury	4.7	7.5
Dursley	2.5	4
North Nibley	4.7	7.5
Wotton-under-Edge	2.2	3.5
Alderley	3.7	6
Somerset Monument	3.1	5
Horton	2.8	4.5
Old Sodbury	2.2	3.5
M4 roundabout	3.1	5
Dyrham Park	2.5	4
Grenville Monument	5.9	9.5
North Stoke	2.2	3.5
Weston	2.5	4
Bath Abbey	2.2	3.5

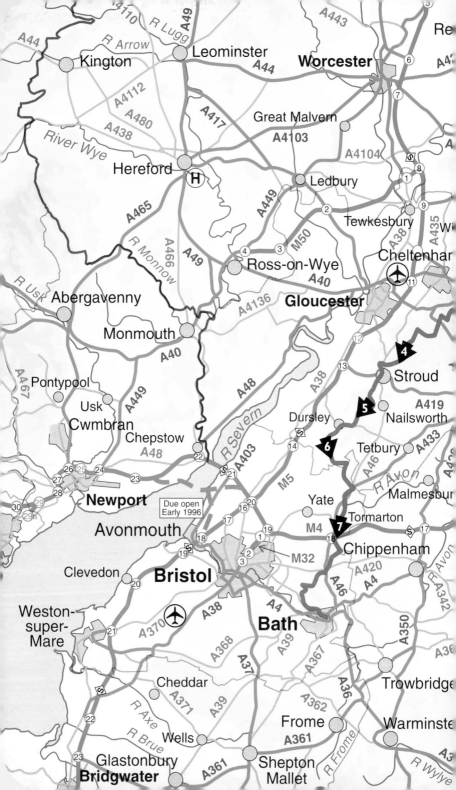

KEY MAP

— Cotswold Way

2 Chapter start point

0 km   10

0 miles   10

INTRODUCTION

Walking the Cotswold Way

It is easy enough to recognise when one is in the Cotswolds: the gentle swell of the upland laced with drystone walls, the nestling villages of rich, creamy stone. It is a good deal more difficult to give precise boundaries to the region. To the east there is a gentle, almost imperceptible rise out of the clays of Northamptonshire and Oxfordshire, so that to those who approach from this direction, the Cotswolds rarely seem like hills at all. There is no sudden dramatic rise, no stern craggy faces, and only rarely do the hills manage to creep over the 1,000 ft mark, generally settling for a more modest elevation. Stripped of earth and grass, the area would be revealed as a vast slab of rock, tilted up from east to west. The one really well-defined boundary comes at this western end, where the Cotswolds meet the Severn valley, and the rock has eroded away to leave a steep escarpment. It is this escarpment that the Cotswold Way follows. But if the boundaries are difficult to set, the unifying factor is easily found in the underlying platform of limestone. This can be seen as pale fragments in the fields or exposed along the escarpment edge; and it is also found in houses, barns and field walls. It is all pervasive.

The limestone of this region is predominantly oolitic. Seen under the microscope, the rock appears full of minute globules like fish roe, and it is from the Greek for 'egg stone' that its name derives. The 'roe' is in fact nothing more than a grain of sand, smoothly coated with calcium carbonate. It is the nature of this rock that gives character to the scenery, as it is worn away in smooth contours to produce the gentle curves in the landscape. Above it the soil is thin and stony, so that the upland is comparatively bare of trees. At one time, it was still more so, for the area was largely given over to sheep grazing. In the eighteenth century, however, landlords dotted the countryside with copses, mainly composed of beech, which remains the dominant tree to this day. In contrast, the deep valleys scored through the plateau are often densely wooded and have a remote, almost mysterious character all their own. Some of these valleys are an enigma, for they no longer carry any trace of river or stream. Two theories have been put forward for this: either the streams have long since found an alternative route, sinking down through fissures in the limestone, or the valleys were not carved by streams at all but were gouged out during the last Ice Age.

The treeless upland has never been the most hospitable of areas, swept by the wind, regularly buried under winter snows, and with little in the way of a water supply to encourage settlement. Not surprisingly, it was in the valleys and hollows that villages and towns were begun and developed through the centuries. Wealth was created in the uplands, based on the grazing sheep with their fine fleeces, but it was in the valleys that the money was spent. Here, villages were constructed of mellow stone, often enriched with churches of a grandeur that seems out of all proportion to the com-

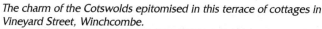

The charm of the Cotswolds epitomised in this terrace of cottages in Vineyard Street, Winchcombe.

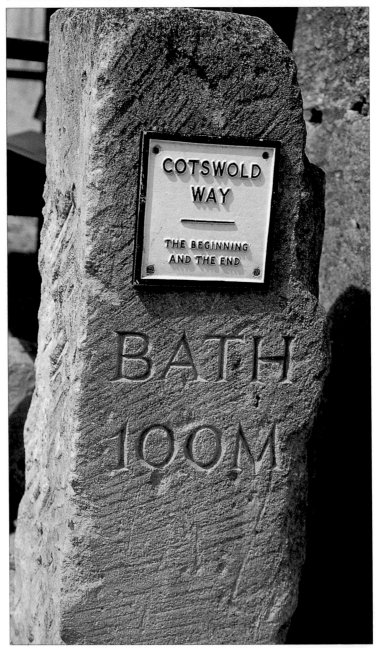

*A plaque in Chipping Campden marks the start of the long-distance walk –
but not quite as long as the stone shows.*

munities they serve. The Cotswold towns and villages represent for many the true English idyll, made all the more attractive by the contrast with the stark uplands. The region sometimes seems so perfect that it might all have been designed as a tourist-board advert. But it was not always so favourably viewed. The famous wit Sydney Smith travelled through the Cotswolds early in the nineteenth century and was not pleased at all with what he found:

> You travel for twenty or five-and-twenty miles over one of the most unfortunate desolate counties under heaven, divided by stone walls, and abandoned to the screaming kites and larcenous crows: after travelling really twenty and to appearances ninety miles over this region of stone and sorrow, life begins to be a burden, and you wish to perish.

He only cheered up when he reached the scarp edge at Birdlip and looked out over the lush Severn valley. It has to be said, however, that Smith was not the greatest enthusiast for the rural life. He wrote in 1838: 'I have no relish for the country; it is a kind of healthy grave.' Very few who walk the Cotswold Way will find themselves sharing his opinions, but all will experience the same delighted astonishment at the 'strikingly sublime' views that suddenly open up along the escarpment.

Today, much of the pleasure of walking in the Cotswolds comes from discovering a world in which nature and man are brought together in close harmony. A drystone wall stands above a ditch from which the stones themselves were dug. The walker will pass a quarry and glance at the exposed stone, and a few minutes later see the same stone used for the farmhouse at the end of the lane; likewise, the stone of the village is that on which the village stands. Some visitors complain that the region is too charming, but it is not the Cotswolds' fault if tourists crowd into the more popular beauty spots. The men who created the settlements did so with no thought of attracting car- and coach-loads of visitors. They used the material that was at hand because it was the sensible, practical thing to do. They built in an unfussy style, largely dictated by the materials they used. They built solidly and well, and time has done the rest. Roofs sag lazily under the weight of centuries; moss and lichen colour and soften what was once hard-edged stone. The charm is not something artificial, but is deep seated and deep rooted in time and place.

The Cotswold Way offers the walker some of the best of the region, and certainly the most dramatic scenery. It also provides an historical perspective and an extraordinary sense of continuity. The techniques

Houses in Whittington showing features characteristic of the Cotswolds: stone wal

...ables, stone tiled roof and dripstone mouldings over mullioned windows.

The village of Sheepscombe huddled beneath the escarpment edge can be visited on the circular walk from Painswick (see p. 80).

employed more than 5,000 years ago, for example, by the people of the New Stone Age, to build drystone walls for their long barrows or burial chambers, were also used to create modern field boundaries. Down through the centuries, changes have left their mark, but seem never to have altered the fundamental character of the area. Even the Industrial Revolution, which transformed so much of Britain, was comfortably absorbed into the Cotswold tradition. It is possible to travel the region and come away unaware that there were once around 150 textile mills at work here. Perhaps this is a clue to the enjoyment to be found by those who walk the Cotswold Way. There is a sense of passing through a landscape that has never broken free of the mould formed many centuries ago. There are occasional interruptions: the M4 certainly comes as a shock to eye and ear. But such intrusions are rare. Sometimes the Cotswolds are described as a 'picture-postcard' area, as though found guilty of some unspecified crime

against modernity. Yet the scenery very rarely falls into smug pretti-
ness, even if the tea shop, the antique shop and, heaven help us, the
gifte shoppe have increasingly taken over from the butcher, the farrier
and the baker. The Cotswolds can cope with that. The landscape is
robust and the villages sturdy, and to walk from one end of the region
to the other is a rare delight.

The first decision that everyone setting out along the Way has to
take is the direction in which to walk. There is no clear-cut 'better'
route. The principal advantage of walking from Bath to Chipping
Campden lies with the weather and the elements. The prevailing
winds of the region are from the south-west, so that those following
this route are likely to have the wind at their backs. They are also
likely in wet weather to avoid the misery of rain in the face, while in
fine weather they will have the advantage of not walking into the sun.
This guide, however, has been written as a description of the route
from north to south. It seems, somehow, perverse to begin the
Cotswold Way with a complex walk up city streets, followed by an
equally complicated meander around the suburbs. Chipping
Campden, by contrast, offers a start which could not be more
Cotswoldian. Another factor which influenced the decision was acces-
sibility. Transport to Chipping Campden is more difficult to organise
than transport to Bath. While it is usually possible to make arrange-
ments for getting to a starting point at a specific time, the end of a
walk is more difficult to predict so that it is all too easy to miss the last
bus. Bath is well served by bus and train, and one can therefore be
fairly certain of getting away with ease at any time. Finally, there is
something to be said for ending a long walk in style, with a sense of
triumph and achievement – and this is something Bath most certainly
provides.

The success of a long-distance walk often depends on the care
taken in the planning and preparation. In this book the route has
been divided into what should be manageable sections, but for those
intending to walk the whole of the Way from end to end, accommodation can be a minor problem. The route tends to avoid towns and
villages, and both camp sites and accommodation are a little thin on
the ground. It is therefore a very good idea to work out each
overnight stop in advance and, for non-campers, advance booking,
whether it is in a guesthouse or in a youth hostel, is advisable, if not
essential. The Ramblers' Association *Cotswold Way Handbook* (see
p. 138) is invaluable, listing most of the accommodation available on
or close to the route. Of course, booking ahead means knowing how
far you can reasonably travel in a day. Do not underestimate the

Almshouses built by Sir Baptist Hicks in the seventeenth century, with the tower of

ipping Campden church in the background.

Cotswolds. This may not be a mountainous area, but there is no shortage of sharp climbs and awkward descents to slow the walker down, and it is better to arrive ahead of schedule, fresh and well, than to trudge on into the dusk, tired and miserable. When it comes to pacing yourself, it is impossible to lay down rules, as individuals have different attitudes and different levels of fitness. Most walkers find that allowing between seven and nine days from end to end makes for a comfortable and pleasant trip. Many, however, will want to allow longer, to pause and enjoy the interesting sites along the route.

Any long-distance walk is made more agreeable if one has the right equipment. Good walking boots are essential, not so much because of steep hills and rough ground, but rather because of mud. In many places, the Cotswold Way follows bridlepaths and, inevitably, horses' hooves cut up the ground. In some places they create a morass which is virtually impossible to get round, offering no alternative but a trudge through almost ankle-deep mud. Good weatherproof clothing is equally essential. The map might suggest that the whole route is little more than a gentle country stroll, but even in summer the wind can whistle over the exposed uplands, bringing cold, driving rain. Winters here can be ferocious; those same winds can pile up snow into deep drifts and it is not unknown for remote Cotswold settlements to be cut off for weeks. This is not meant to be alarmist. The great majority of walkers will enjoy a trouble-free journey, but it is common sense to prepare for the worst likely conditions. If they do not arrive then nothing is lost; if they do, then being ready for them can make the difference between pleasure and misery or worse.

All the normal rules of country walking apply in the Cotswolds: have your maps with you and a compass – and if you do not know how to use the latter, find out. Plan your days carefully: you will often find that there is no suitable stop for refreshments, so carry your own food and, most importantly, drink. Tell someone where you are going, as accidents can happen, and no one wants to be left lying in a field or wood with a broken ankle, hoping that perhaps they will be missed. In the end, it comes down to common sense. A walk along the Cotswold Way is not a Himalayan trek, but good planning and sensible precautions are as advisable for one as they are for the other. Take a little time to think ahead and you can be sure of enjoying a magnificent long-distance walk.

The charming village of Snowshill shows just how beautifully the buildings harmonise with the surrounding countryside.

COTSWOLD STONE

The builders of the Cotswold area were doubly blessed: the local stone has a rare beauty and is easily worked, being relatively soft when taken from the quarry. This encouraged the local masons to shape it into smooth-faced blocks for even the most modest buildings and to add rich decorative details to the grandest. The style that is now considered typical of the Cotswolds owes everything to the nature of the stone. Because this was so readily available even cottages were given an ashlar façade, one in which the stone is dressed to create a smooth front. Again, instead of having to skimp on materials on the upper floors by using dormer windows let into the roof, the Cotswold builder could extend the walls upwards into gables. The ease of carving is reflected in the tall, shaped chimneys, mullioned windows and, most characteristically, in the dripstone mouldings above the windows. These are the basic elements of the Cotswold house, but there are endless variations and elaborations. Shapely finials stand above gables, doorways are surrounded by elaborate mouldings and, in the grander houses, details such as coats of arms are added. But whatever the design, cottage and manor share in the same splendour that derives from the stone itself. The limestone seems not so much to reflect the light as to absorb and throw it back, enriched with a deep, golden glow. Above all, the use of local stone creates a resonance between the houses and the ground on which they stand. One could not imagine the traditional Cotswold house being at home in any other region.

Cotswold stone is not used only for the façades of buildings. Some types of limestone are fissile, i.e. capable of being split into layers. This is the origin of the material variously known as 'stone slates' or, more often in this area, 'stone tiles'. Such tiles were used for roofing, and it is the combination of stone walls and stone roof which produces the finest buildings in the Cotswolds. Traditionally, the stones were quarried, then laid out in winter and watered every day. All that was needed to split them was a hard frost and a quick thaw. An ordinary modern roof is built up of tiles of uniform size and thickness, but to construct a Cotswold roof, stone tiles were roughly graded in size, with the smallest placed nearest to the ridge, and the largest at the eaves. The different sizes each had their own name, such as muffities, wiretts and tauts. There were no precise measurements and, as a result, no two Cotswold roofs are ever quite the same. A rare opportunity to see the underside of a stone roof is provided by the market hall at Chipping Campden. Here one can see the size and shape of the individual stone tiles, and how they are fixed to the battens by wooden pegs. The Cotswold house needed to be sturdy to support its roof, which weighed around 1 ton per 100 square feet (1 tonne per 9 square metres). Yet the overall effect is one of great charm, and it would be a hard-hearted soul who did not respond to this poem in stone.

ARCHAEOLOGY

Remains have been found in the Cotswolds dating back to the Neolithic or New Stone Age, which lasted from around 4,000 to 2,000 BC. There are traces of a settlement at Crickley Hill, but the Neolithic camp here was abandoned then reinhabited around 700 BC, when the defences were greatly strengthened. To obtain a glimpse of the culture of our distant ancestors, one has to turn to the tombs they built for the dead. Known as long barrows, these tombs are virtually identical to others found in South Wales, indicating how the early farming communities gradually made their way eastward across the Severn to the Cotswolds and onward into what is now Oxfordshire. There are many examples of such tombs, and two of the finest are to be seen near the Cotswold Way: Belas Knap and Hetty Pegler's Tump. In both cases, the stone burial chambers are covered by huge grassy mounds, and each has an impressive forecourt with delicate stone walls that lead to a false entrance. The actual entrance to the tomb is in the side of the mound. These two sites were used for many burials – 38 skeletons were unearthed at Belas Knap and there may originally have been more. One can only guess at the nature of the religion which made such elaborate burials necessary.

The Stone Age ended with the introduction of metals, and around 2,000 BC saw the beginning of the Bronze Age. Burial mounds can again be found dating from this period, although this time they are round barrows. There are two rather insignificant examples near the Cotswold Way. With the arrival of the Iron Age, around 500 BC, came a period of great activity, characterised by inter-tribal rivalry. The people defended themselves by constructing hill-forts, typically choosing an upland summit or promontory. They improved on the natural defences offered by the steep hillsides by excavating deep ditches and using the rock and soil to build high ramparts. There are several examples along the Way, of which the forts of Uley and Painswick are the best.

The Iron Age hill-forts were stalwart defences for as long as the people were fighting among themselves, but they offered little protection against the steady encroachment of the Roman armies, which first arrived in Britain in 55 BC. Cirencester was then Corinium Dobunnorum, the regional capital of the Dobunni, and stood at the heart of a network of roads: Fosse Way, Akeman and Ermine Streets. It also became an artistic centre, famous for its mosaicists. The Romans clearly liked the region and settled here, establishing a number of rich villas. The word 'villa' today suggests a modest suburban house, but these were large farms, often with luxurious living quarters. There would be mosaic pavements in the main rooms, bath houses and a hypocaust or central-heating system. They were the stately homes of their day. The Way runs past Witcombe villa, but there are far grander examples in the Cotswolds at Chedworth and North Leigh. The museum at Cirencester has many outstanding Roman remains on display.

The Roman baths in Bath with the Abbey in the background: the southern end of the Cotswold Way.

ABBEYS AND CHURCHES

There are few imposing monastic remains in the Cotswolds, but this does not mean that there were no grand abbeys or that the Church was not influential in the region. The abbeys were among the most powerful landowners and by the end of the thirteenth century the abbey of Gloucester had a flock of 10,000 sheep roaming the Cotswolds. An equally large flock belonged to the more modest abbey at Winchcombe. These and most other monastic houses were destroyed during the reign of Henry VIII. They were sold off to private owners who used the stones to build great mansions and turned the grounds into parkland. The remains of Hailes Abbey give an idea of its extent and wealth, while a sixteenth-century gatehouse is the only surviving fragment of Kingswood Abbey, its elaborate carving hinting at the opulence that has been lost.

The great abbey church that marks one end of the Cotswold Way straddles the decades either side of Henry VIII's dissolution of the monasteries. Bath Abbey was founded in 1499 and was left unfinished during Henry's reign, its stained-glass windows vandalised, its roof stripped of lead. Work began again under Elizabeth I and was finally completed in the seventeenth century.

The abbeys owed much of their wealth to their ownership of great flocks and of the land on which they grazed. The churches in turn benefited from the generosity of clothiers and wool merchants, who spent a good deal of their fortunes on church buildings. William Grevel, who died in 1401, is described in his memorial brass as 'the flower of the wool merchants of all England'. He left 100 marks towards the rebuilding of Chipping Campden church. Others were no less generous, and the result is a succession of churches built or extended during the late-medieval period, in the style known as Perpendicular. It is easy to see how the name came about. Everywhere the emphasis is on the vertical: on tall towers, on decorative details such as mouldings that run from floor to roof and, most importantly, on immense high windows. Chipping Campden perfectly demonstrates those qualities. Anyone wanting to see the finest of the other wool churches must stray off the Cotswold Way – to Fairford, for example, with its astonishing array of medieval stained glass, or to Burford, where generations of merchants added to and beautified the church. Grandest of them all, however, is Cirencester, with its gorgeously ornate tower and its even more majestic Gothic porch, extending up through three full storeys.

The cloister arches, almost all that remains of the once-magnificent buildings of

Hailes Abbey.

Walkers on the Cotswold Way should make sure to include one memorable church – or rather churchyard – in their itinerary. The approach to Painswick church is down paths lined with yew trees planted at the end of the eighteenth century – 99 of them in all. Beyond is perhaps the most remarkable and handsome collection of carved tombs to be found anywhere in England.

THE ARTS AND CRAFTS MOVEMENT

The Arts and Crafts movement was begun in the nineteenth century as a reaction to the filth, squalor and degradation that seemed to be inseparable from the relentless advance of industrialisation. In fine art it was closely allied to the Pre-Raphaelite call for a return to nature as the only true inspiration for art. For the craftsman it represented a turning away from over-elaborate design and from the world of machines. One of the great leaders of the movement was William Morris, poet, architect, textile and book designer, and much else. He expressed his personal philosophy as follows:

> Never forget the material you are working with, and try always to use it for what it can do best; if you feel yourself hampered by the material in which you are working, instead of being helped by it, you have so far not learned your business, any more than a would-be poet has, who complains of the hardship of writing in measure and rhyme.

Not surprisingly, Morris fell in love with the Cotswolds, an area where tradition survived and where buildings perfectly demonstrate respect for local materials. With his friends Dante Gabriel Rossetti and Edward Burne-Jones, he often stayed in Broadway Tower, and in 1871 he took a lease on Kelmscott Manor, a name which became famous through the beautifully produced books of the Kelmscott Press.

Morris was no mere theorist; 'The Firm' he established produced a range of products from wallpapers to stained-glass windows (examples of the latter can be seen in Selsey church, near Stroud). He had a number of enthusiastic disciples, including Ernest Gimson, who set up his Daneway workshops at Sapperton in 1902, making hand-crafted furniture. Gimson's modestly stated aim was to produce work that was 'useful and right, pleasantly shaped and finished, good enough, but not too good for ordinary use'. In fact, his craftsmen created furniture which stands proudly in a great English tradition. Other craftsmen, too, made their way to the Cotswolds. In 1902 C.R. Ashbee arrived in Chipping Campden with an entire London guild of

Sudeley Castle, once the home of Katherine Parr, sixth wife of Henry VIII. It was restored in the last century.

handicraft workers, 150 people in all, and moved into premises in Sheep Street.

William Morris's concern for craftsmanship, materials and tradition extended beyond making beautiful things for his contemporaries. He was an equally passionate defender of the beauties of the past. The Victorian age saw a great rush towards the 'restoration' of ancient churches, but all too often this led to the destruction of original features, which were hidden behind the elaborate curlicues and twiddles of the new Gothic. The result, wrote Morris, was to make an old church look like 'a nineteenth-century medieval furniture-dealer's warehouse'. He believed restoration should be limited to keeping out the wet and ensuring the walls remained upright. To promote his ideas he founded The Society for the Protection of Ancient Buildings. It is thanks to Morris and his successors that many of the Cotswold churches have been spared from the heavy hand of the restorer.

WOOL AND CLOTH

The thirteenth century saw a great expansion in sheep-rearing, the impetus coming from across the Channel in Flanders, where a thriving cloth industry was demanding more and more wool. Land that had once been ploughed for crops was turned back to grass and grazed by the sturdy Cotswold sheep. The demand from Flanders declined during the next century, but by now the wool merchants were rich enough and confident enough to begin cloth manufacture on their own account. The area was ideally situated. There was ample grazing and clear water for washing fleeces. The humid climate was ideal for working the wool into yarn and weaving it into cloth. The finished cloth was treated with fuller's earth, plentifully available in the region, then pounded in water to shrink and felt it, creating a tight weave. Originally, this was done by men walking up and down on the cloth (the origin of the common surname Walker). After fulling, the nap of the cloth was raised using spiky teazle heads, again widely available in the Cotswolds, then cut smooth with shears. It could be sold as white cloth, or coloured using local dyes such as woad. In time, the Stroud area became famous for its scarlet cloth. The finished cloth was sent on its way from what was then Britain's second-busiest port, Bristol.

At first, cloth-making was very much a cottage industry, dependent on vast numbers of home spinners and hand-loom weavers. Gradually, however, mechanisation was introduced. This began in medieval times with the fulling mill, in which giant hammers, powered by a water wheel, did the job of the walkers. Next the raising of the nap was transformed: the teazles were mounted on drums, again powered by water wheel. Soon textile mills were spreading out along every available stream. The greatest changes came in the eighteenth century, when the spinning wheel of the cottage was replaced by the machinery of the mill, and, inevitably, the power loom took over from the hand loom. The early mills were often indistinguishable in their outward appearance from the older, grain mills, with the same busy water wheel and simple stone building with stone-slate roof.

The nineteenth century brought a new source of power, the steam engine, but the water wheel was far from redundant. One of the grandest of the new generation of mills was Stanley Mill at King's Stanley, which was built in 1813 with five water wheels and just one steam engine. It was worked in partnership with nearby Ebley Mill, built in the style of a French chateau. Stanley Mill was still producing textiles in the early 1990s, but Ebley has been converted into council offices.

The decline of the woollen industry began in the late nineteenth century. High tariffs made it harder to sell cloth abroad and there was increasingly fierce competition from the highly mechanised, modern mills of Yorkshire. One by one the woollen mills closed. Along the southern section of the Cotswold Way there are many fine old mill buildings to be seen, with their mill ponds and sluices. Sadly the rattle of loom and shuttle has now all but vanished from the Cotswold valleys.

OLD WAYS AND TRACKS

The Cotswold Way seems to follow an obvious line directly related to the natural contours of the land, keeping very much to the edge of the escarpment. The same is true of the main prehistoric trackways, which also kept to the ridges, well clear of the heavy clays and dense undergrowth of the valleys. The so-called Jurassic Way follows the high ground all the way from the Avon valley to the Humber. Because this was a natural route rather than a man-made road, the evidence for its use is scant, but it is thought to have left the Avon valley via Lansdown Hill, and to have continued on past Cold Ashton and the hill-fort of Little Sodbury to head off towards Stow-on-the-Wold.

The Romans, when they arrived, paid little heed to natural geography. Their roads were famous for going straight from place to place and the routes can still be followed today. Roman roads were built with care, raised up on a bank or aggar with drainage ditches on

Cattle grazing at Wresden Farm near Dursley. Downham Hill can be seen in the

background.

either side, and surfaced with stone and gravel. Ryknild Street, which ran from the Cotswolds into Staffordshire, crosses the walk near Chipping Campden, while the Ermine Way climbs the scarp face near Birdlip. Neither road, however, has made as great an impact on the landscape as have the major routes centred on Cirencester. Perhaps the greatest tribute that can be paid to the Roman builders is the fact that modern engineers have found no better routes for their own roads than those laid down by their predecessors, working nearly 2,000 years ago.

The period following the collapse of the Roman Empire is known as the Dark Ages, but it was not a time of unremitting anarchy. Trade continued, especially in such essential commodities as salt, which was vital for preserving meat. As early as the eighth century AD, the King of Mercia had granted the church at Worcester a plot of ground for salt houses in Droitwich. Radiating from this point were a number of roads, known as the salt ways. One of these routes passed close to Winchcombe, and is still remembered in the names Salter's Lane and Salter's Hill. Another old route in the same area was the Pilgrims' Way, built in the Middle Ages to link the abbeys of Hailes and Winchcombe. Originally it was paved, and walkers who come this way along what is often an exceedingly muddy track may well wish that it still was.

Some old routes are more distinct than others. No one can be certain when the drove roads that linked England to Wales first came into use, but it might well have been as long ago as Norman times. Such roads remained in use until the railways took over the job of moving cattle from Wales to England in the nineteenth century. The herds were slowly moved out from the Welsh hills to be fattened on the lusher pastures of the English Midlands before being sold. One drove road followed the old line of Ermine Street, then set off up the escarpment from the village of Great Witcombe, below the Cotswold Way at Birdlip. It must have been an impressive sight to see the great herds slowly winding their way up the steep hillside.

The Cotswold Way is a comparatively new creation, but throughout its length there are reminders of routes whose use can be traced back through many centuries.

THE
COTSWOLD
WAY

1 CHIPPING CAMPDEN TO WINCHCOMBE

via Broadway and Hailes Abbey   *17 ½ miles (25 km)*

There could scarcely be a better example of a Cotswold town than Chipping Campden, but to start at the official beginning of the Way is to miss the best of it. So this description starts a few hundred yards back, and surely no one could complain at the extra walking involved.

The church of St James **1** is one of those glorious Perpendicular churches, paid for out of the profits of a thriving wool trade. It is approached along an avenue of lime trees, six to each side, representing the twelve Apostles. Both inside and out, the eye is constantly drawn upwards – by the strong verticals of the mouldings on the tower, and by the shimmering richness of decoration, particularly on the tombs. The alabaster effigies of Sir Baptist and Lady Elizabeth Hicks present a picture of grandeur, frozen and immortalised.

Leaving the church, one finds a wealth of fine architecture on view. Over to the left is the very ornate entrance to what was once Sir Baptist Hicks's house. Built in 1613, it was destroyed by retreating Royalists in the Civil War: 'the house which was so faire, burnt', as one account records. All that remains is the Banqueting House, a riot of pinnacles and gables. Opposite are the modest, but no less attractive, almshouses. The miracle of Chipping Campden is that so many styles can live so comfortably together, unified by the local stone and a long tradition. Bedford House with its pilasters, cornices and cheeky cherubs does not look out of place, even when set against fourteenth-century buildings such as Grevel House and Woolstaplers' Hall. In the main street is a last reminder of Sir Baptist Hicks: the market hall **2** he endowed. Shortly after this comes the more modern Catholic church, and it is here that the Cotswold Way has its official start **A**.

Turn up the side street by the church and, where the road swings round to the right, turn left past a very attractive thatched cottage. At the end of the road continue on up the rough track, past an orchard on the left. Cross the stile by the farm buildings and continue uphill on the narrow footpath. This early part of the walk is like the overture to some major work, introducing all the themes that will be developed later. Having left the ideal Cotswold town, one is now introduced to Cotswold farmland, fields speckled with stone. Turn left at the road and, a hundred yards on, turn right to continue along the footpath at the side of the hedge, which leads up to the grassland at the top of the escarpment. Here is one of those magnificent panoramas which are such a feature of the Cotswold Way, looking out across the Vale of Evesham. Equally typical is the fact that this is a place with a story to tell. Around 1612 Robert Dover instituted annual games here at Dover's Hill, under the grand title of the Olympick Games; they lasted with a few breaks right through to the nineteenth century.

At the end of the field, the walk turns left to follow the line of the hedge over a wide expanse of turf. Along the way is a topograph **3** – again, the first of many – indicating what can be seen in the surrounding landscape. At the end of the grassland, go through the car park to the roadway and turn left; the next major objective on the walk, Broadway Tower, now comes into view. At the crossroads turn right. About half a mile down the road, in the trees, is the Kiftsgate Stone **4**, which marks a moot or meeting place, where locals gathered to discuss affairs as far back as Saxon times. Where the road bends round to the right by a small copse **B**, turn left across the stile and follow the footpath that swings round to the right. Here it joins the Mile Drive, a

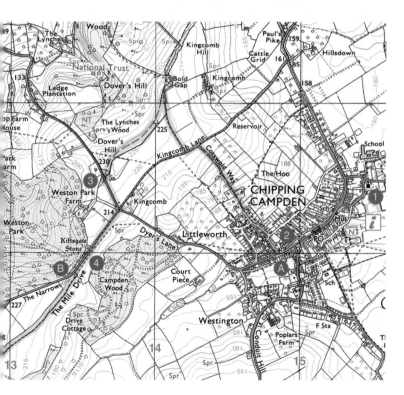

The waymarked and clearly defined path cutting across a field of poppies on the

plateau above Broadway.

broad grassy track like some great processional way. Over to the left is a view of Campden House and its surrounding parkland. Where the broad track turns off to the left, continue straight on over the stone stile and across the field to the obvious gap in the stone wall. At the next wall, head directly towards the top of Broadway Tower, which can be seen peeping over the horizon. This is very much a plateau, bare and windswept, dotted with stunted trees. Cross the road and continue straight on towards the Fish Inn, turning right at the stile. Here there is a panorama dial, with a bas-relief map of the surrounding area. The Way goes round the panorama; just before the road, turn right to follow the line of the road, then left to follow the path through a little area of woodland. Cross straight over the busy road and continue on the footpath up a grassy bank to join a broad track. Near the top of the bank, by a little quarry, turn right to follow the path through the patch of woodland. Cross the stile by the wooden gate and continue straight on over open grassland. The track is quite well defined, and is waymarked by posts with yellow arrows. Soon the tower itself appears in view; it is approached along a little dry valley, from which one emerges to be faced by one of the great panoramic views of the Cotswold Way. Go through the gate in the stone wall to the tower.

Broadway Tower, one of the best viewpoints along the Way.

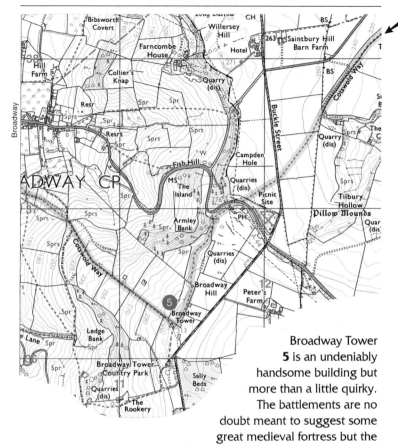

Broadway Tower **5** is an undeniably handsome building but more than a little quirky. The battlements are no doubt meant to suggest some great medieval fortress but the round-headed windows and dainty balconies give it an almost cosy air. The view from the top is scarcely different from that at the bottom, so why was it built? The answer, as with so many follies, would seem to be to impress the neighbours. It was constructed around 1800 to a design by James Wyatt for the Earl of Coventry, but the Countess seems to have been the enthusiast behind the scheme. It was said that before construction began she ordered a beacon to be lit on the top of the hill, and was then driven throughout the surrounding countryside to make sure everyone could see it. The tower is open to visitors.

The walk continues downhill, following the line of the wire fence, past some fine old beech trees. The escarpment now falls away quite steeply and walking is made easier by a short flight of steps. The path continues past a recently restored drystone wall. Having crossed the stile by the wooden gate, do not take the broad track that swings

Cottages in Broadway, with little dormer windows instead of the gables of grander houses.

round to the right, but continue straight on across the grassland, as shown by the line of posts. Over to the right is a fine example of ridge and furrow. In medieval times, fields were divided into narrow strips, and as the same strip was ploughed over and over again, so the ridges grew ever higher. When at a later date the field was grassed and turned over to pasture, the old pattern was retained as if in a fossilised landscape. At the bottom of the hill, the path goes through a gap in the hedgerow and turns diagonally to the right towards the lower edge of a patch of conifers. Continue across the small stream bordered by willow and go down a little lane which comes out in the wide main street of Broadway **6**.

Turn left down the street, which is one of the showpieces of the Cotswolds. It is a tourist honey-pot, but one has to remember that tourists come because it really does have a wealth of fine buildings. The overall effect is very impressive, but often it is the individual building – or even the small detail – that catches the eye. No. 68, for example, has an unusual little porch supported on classical pillars. Houses vary from those in the local style to others with gentrified, bland ashlar frontages. At the Broadway Hotel, which incorporates an old timber-framed section, turn left onto the Snowshill road. It goes past very grand Bannits House, with neat topiary, and a romantic thatched cottage. Turn right opposite another house with even grander topiary **C** to follow the broad track. Just before the drive to the cottage, turn left to go through the gate and continue on to the bridge across the stream.

There is now a fine, open prospect. The path crosses a little bridge made out of railway sleepers and continues up the field to the stile by the road. Cross this stile and the one opposite to take the path beside the hedge, which seems a popular nesting place for a variety of birds, including chaffinch, greenfinch, robin and wren. At the end of the narrow footpath, continue following the line of the hedge up to the wood, and then follow the edge of the woodland round to the left. Enter the woods by the wooden gate and continue on along the track between the trees, a mixture of oak, ash, birch and coppiced hazel. At the top of the little hill, turn left onto the broader track and leave the wood by another wooden gate, emerging onto arable land. Follow the track between the edge of the wood and the field and carry straight on. As the hedge thins out, Broadway Tower appears over to the left. Continue on the same line to the barn. Immediately beyond the barn, turn right across two stiles, then turn left onto the broad farm track **D**.

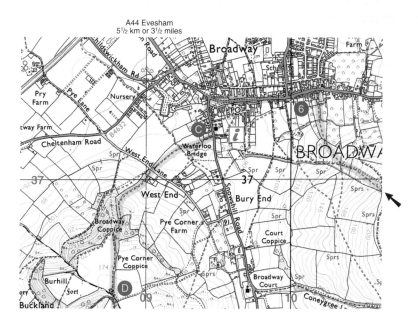

This plateau of farmland seems alternately to echo with the song of skylarks and the less pleasant howl of low-flying jet fighters. At the top of the little hill, cross two stiles by the farm buildings and turn right through the gate to continue following the broad track **E**. At the end of a line of beech, continue straight on up the hill. This is pleasant, easy walking with wide views out over the Vale of Evesham. The path swings round to the left, past the remains of an old quarry. Another large quarry appears at the top of the hill.

Here a number of tracks meet. On the left is Snowshill, which may be visited on the circular walk (see p. 53). Cross over the cattle grid to take the track on the right that goes through a most attractive area of smooth turf studded with trees, and passes yet another old quarry on the left. The path leads to the rather insubstantial embankments that mark the edge of Shenberrow Camp, an Iron Age settlement. At Shenberrow Buildings, go through the iron gate and follow the track downhill along the hollow, its sides brightened by hawthorn and gorse. Where the path divides, take the track to the left, going downhill by the post with the yellow arrow. Cross the stile in the wall and turn right to continue downhill. The village of Stanton now comes into view at the bottom of the valley. The path swings round to the right through a gateway and over a stile to continue on the other side of the wall, and drops down into a small, closed-in valley with a reservoir at the bottom. It then runs along the top of the reservoir and across a stile to what can be an exceedingly muddy lane through woodland. This is mercifully short and emerges to a broad track. Turn left towards Stanton, past a lovely pair of cottages, built in stone with high, thatched roofs, through which little dormer windows peer. The lane emerges at the green in the centre of Stanton. Thirsty – or hungry – walkers can turn right to visit the Mount Inn, but the Cotswold Way sternly resists temptation, going down the village street to the left.

Stanton is one of those places one hesitates to write about or even mention too loudly, for it has a fragile charm that could all too easily be broken. Here, if anywhere, one feels at the very heart of the Cotswolds, for Stanton has a wealth of superb buildings and not a whiff of pretension. At first sight the church **7** is something of a jumble, both of styles and levels, with odd features such as the dormer window in the roof, and the gargoyles. Inside, there is a surprising serenity and unity, with more grotesque carvings on pillars, an organ loft and rood screen. (See p. 52 for the circular walk beginning from the centre of Stanton.) Beyond the market cross and the church are the imposing gates that lead to Stanton Court. Turn left at the road.

Where the road turns round to the right, continue straight on along the track to Chestnut Farm, then turn right over the stile into the field and continue on along the obvious track. A pattern of old ridges and furrows can be seen in the field. Follow the path beside the broad farm track, cross the stile and continue diagonally to the right towards the isolated oak tree. Over to the right is a long viaduct, which once carried the Gloucestershire and Warwickshire Railway, built as part of the Great Western empire in an attempt to ward off territorial attacks by a rival company, the Midland. The occasional blast of a steam whistle echoing across the fields indicates that the line is not all disused – a section has been reopened as a preserved line, with ambitious plans for future expansion. This is now a very pleasant walk over grassland, with the Way marked by wooden posts. Farmland gradually merges into formal parkland with its carefully arranged, yet apparently artless, pattern of fields, hedges and trees. The track heads slightly right to join the road near a little

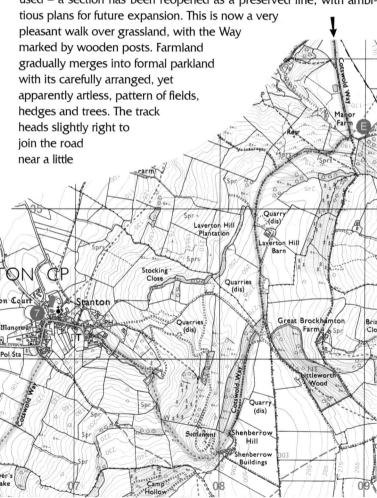

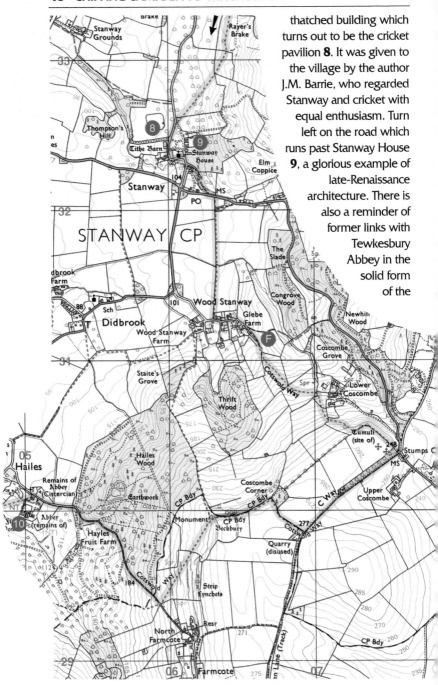

thatched building which turns out to be the cricket pavilion **8**. It was given to the village by the author J.M. Barrie, who regarded Stanway and cricket with equal enthusiasm. Turn left on the road which runs past Stanway House **9**, a glorious example of late-Renaissance architecture. There is also a reminder of former links with Tewkesbury Abbey in the solid form of the great buttressed tithe barn. Among the other outbuildings is the brew-house, which has recently been brought back into use; its excellent ale is available in a few local pubs. Follow the road as it swings round towards the formal entrance to the house. This structure features a whole array of architectural devices, including columns, pilasters, pediments and niches. Next to it the church is more modest but still has lovely detail: just look, for example, at the carved heads, which include one very smug-looking gentleman with an upturned moustache. There is a particularly good view of the house (occasionally open to the public) from the churchyard. Another feature of the village is the war monument with crisp lettering by the brilliant typographer and carver Eric Gill.

Beyond the gateway, turn left by the tree with a bench around the trunk to pass the Stanway Estate Yard. Cross over the road, turning slightly left to take the path opposite that leads in a straight line across the fields and over a succession of stiles. On the right is a distant view of the preserved railway at Didbrook. Turn left on the road through Wood Stanway and follow it as it bends to the right, past a farm and pony-trekking centre **F**. Continue straight on past the barns and follow the rough track as it begins to climb uphill, back to the top of the escarpment, waymarked by wooden posts. Once through the wooden gate in the wall, just before the farm buildings, turn right, again head-ing for the wooden post. Cross the big ladder stile and continue fol-lowing the broad farm track for 100 yards, then turn diagonally right onto the path that heads uphill past a solitary tree. At the top of the hill, turn left along the path beside the stone wall and the line of beech trees, which are home to a clamorous rookery. By the roadway is the stump of a cross, hence the name Stumps Cross. Go over the stile to join the road, then immediately turn right onto the bridleway that runs by an avenue of trees. At the end of the avenue is a corrugated barn, looking slightly incongruous perched high on staddle-stones. The Way continues in a long straight, then turns right at a farm gate. Over to the left are the obvious ramparts of a small hill-fort. Continue to the left round the edge of the field; one can now see how the escarpment pro-vides a more impressive defence than the earthworks. Carry on to the stone pillar, after which the path heads steeply downhill through the trees towards the gate in the wooden fence. At the stile by the signpost near the woodland, turn right to follow the bridleway that runs between the woodland and the orchard. At the end of the track, continue straight on along the roadway. We are here back in the Vale and, after a good deal of climbing up and down the escarpment, are now just a mile away from Wood Stanton. The Way, has, however, arrived at one of its most important historic sites, Hailes Abbey **10**. This is open to the

Snowshill Manor, a splendid Tudor building and home to an eccentric collection of antiques.

public, although there is a very good view of the site from the walk. One reason to visit the abbey is the small but excellent museum which, apart from telling the history of the buildings, has a fascinating exhibition showing the variety of the local stones, ranging from steely blue lias to the familiar golden oolitic limestone. The abbey was founded in the middle of the thirteenth century, and was one of the last Cistercian houses in England. Now all that remains are a row of cloister arches, part of the chapter house and the foundations telling of a once-great array of buildings. The little church opposite could easily be overlooked, but inside is a splendid set of medieval wall paintings.

Turn left opposite Hailes church, through the wooden gate, and head on a diagonal to the right towards the gate in the corner. Isolated stone fragments and humps in the ground indicate outlying abbey remains. Continue on the gravel path, past the houses, and turn right onto the road. As the road turns round to the right, turn left onto the bridleway, part of the old Pilgrims' Way. As you begin to go uphill, turn right by a wooden post with a yellow arrow, onto the track that runs past an old and massive oak tree. The path turns left through the copse and continues on to cross a small stream before joining a narrow lane, which opens out to a broad track between hedges. At the roadway turn left, and there follows a short suburban trudge before the older buildings of Winchcombe appear.

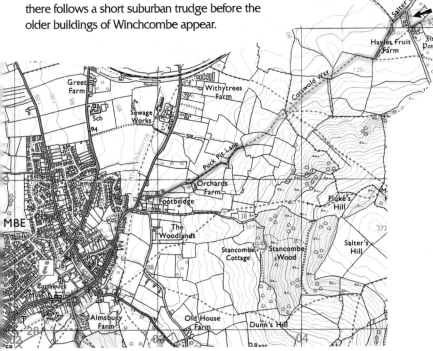

CIRCULAR WALK FROM STANTON

6½ miles (10 km)

The walk begins at the cross in the centre of Stanton. Take the public footpath into the churchyard and go round the east end of the church **7** to leave by the narrow path between stone walls. At the end of the path, do not cross the stile but turn left beside the railings. Go through the kissing gate, over the plank bridge and turn left. This footpath leads to the village of Laverton. Turn right at the road to reach the village green and the old school with its bell tower. Cross the road and continue straight on along the bridleway, across farmland.

At the roadway, turn right into the delightful little village of Buckland **11**, where the fifteenth-century rectory provides an imposing introduction to the broad street of attractive houses. The old manor house (now a hotel) stands next to the church, which has most unusual seventeenth-century canopied seating around the walls. The medieval glass was restored by William Morris. Beyond the church, the road swings round to the left, but the walk continues straight on along the footpath that climbs the grassy bank.

Cross the stile and carry on up the field, turning back for a fine view of the church and manor. Go through another stile by an iron gate, beyond which the route is indicated by yellow arrows on prominent posts. Continue steadily uphill. Near the top, where the wooden fence is crossed by a stile, turn left, go through the metal gate and head for the post with the arrow on the brow of the hill opposite. Go through the metal gate at the end of the wood and follow the broad track round to the right.

The view on the other side of the hill is very different from that across the Severn plain. There is now a valley surrounded by generously curved hills, darkened by patches of conifer. Continue to follow the metalled road beside the wood and, just beyond the edge of the conifers, turn left through the gate by the footpath sign, heading down a steep hill **A**. At the bottom of the hill cross the stile and take the path through the wood. Leave by the footbridge and wooden gate, and turn slightly to the right to go uphill, as indicated by the arrow, keeping the old oak tree to the left. At the next prominent group of oaks turn right over the stile and head for a point to the left of the house. At the stile at the top of the hill, join the road and turn right to Snowshill. Where the road divides keep to the right.

Snowshill is among the most picturesque of Cotswold villages. Snowshill Manor **12**, now owned by the National Trust, houses one of the country's most eccentric collections, containing everything from Samurai armour to dolls' prams. Continue on past the Snowshill Arms and the church and take the road out of the village, going uphill past a small wood. Just before the brow of the hill, turn right onto the road marked as a dead end. Where this divides, go straight on and, as the road turns sharply to the right, turn left by a bridleway sign. Go into the field and continue diagonally to the post visible on the horizon. Follow the same route across the next field. At the broad track, turn left, then immediately right by the gatepost with the blue arrow. At the house where three pathways meet **B**, turn left to take the bridleway that runs along the edge of the wood. At the next iron gate continue straight downhill. Go through the gate at the end, and turn slightly right to follow the bridleway down towards Stanton. Along the hillside the humps and hollows of old quarries can still be seen. The path reaches the edge of the village at the Cotswold Way. Continue down the village street. At the junction by the small war memorial turn right to return to the start.

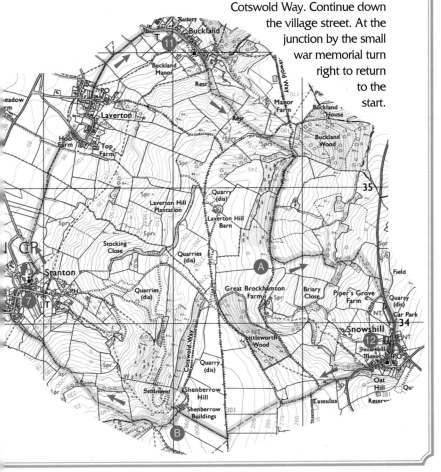

2 WINCHCOMBE TO DOWDESWELL

via Belas Knap   *11 miles (18 km)*

Winchcombe has buildings not just of great character, but of great variety. Timber-framed houses stand next to others of substantial stone. The Corner Cupboard is not an antique shop, but a very pleasant old inn, while the George, which was once a galleried inn, is now a private house. Queen's Square has the best of the secular architecture in the Jacobean House, built in 1619. Inevitably the grandest building is the church **13**, another example of the Perpendicular style, with its typical clerestory windows. Outside is a fearsome array of gargoyles; strange beasts snarl down while monsters with hideous faces glower out over the churchyard. These mythological horrors were once matched in real life: bullet marks show where Royalist prisoners were lined up and shot in the Civil War. The interior of the church contains a particularly fine polychrome monument, in a delightful naive style, to Thomas Williams, buried in 1636. The town also has an interesting local museum and a wonderfully bizarre railway museum.

Beyond Queens Square **A**, turn left down Vineyard Street (once known as Duck Street as there was a ducking stool by the river at the bottom). Across the bridge is a barn, packed with ecclesiastical details, which might well have come from the old abbey after the dissolution. At the gateway **14** to Sudeley Castle, which is the start of a circular walk (see p. 64), take the road round to the right and then turn right through an iron kissing gate. Turn diagonally to the left towards the telegraph pole with the Footpath sign. From here there is a clear pathway through the arable field, and a good view across to Sudeley Castle. Continue on to cross a bridge over a stream and follow the path to the right round the edge of the field. Once over the stile, continue along the hedge. The walk now goes over rough grassland and, as it steadily climbs, so the view keeps improving. The route is briefly closed in, running up a narrow lane between the hedge and the iron fence. As the hill levels out, the track reaches Wadfield Farm and winds on up the hill towards Humblebee Cottages.

At the roadway turn right. The road passes through the edge of woodland dominated by larch and ash, which are popular with the local woodpeckers. Turn left across a stile onto the footpath signposted to Belas Knap. Once through the woods turn left along the line of the

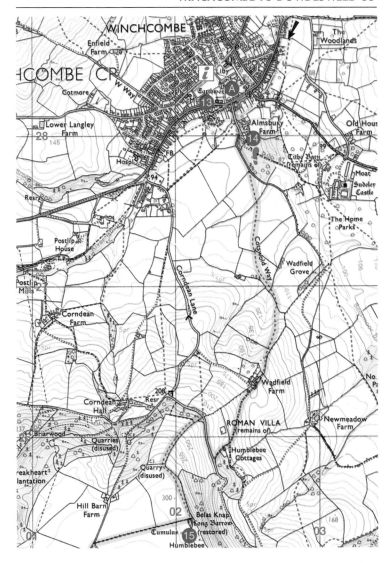

fence and continue on round the edge of the field. Pass through the kissing gate and follow the boundary wall of a dense and tangled wood. The high mound of Belas Knap long barrow **15** rears up ahead. The loneliness of the location adds to the drama of this New Stone Age burial mound. The impressive drystone walls sweep in towards what turns out to be a false entrance, blocked by a stone; the actual burial chambers are to be found at the sides. The people who lived here some

The mellow charms of Winchcombe, a village that stands on the little River Isbourn

The Neolithic long barrow of Belas Knap. The impressive 'entrance' is, in fact, fake; the actual entrances to the tomb are at the sides.

4,000 years ago have left no written records, but Belas Knap is an eloquent testament to their skills and craftsmanship.

Leave the enclosure by the stile. One now returns to the landscape of the plateau, with extensive fields neatly divided by stone walls. At the end of a rather dull trudge beside fields, join the broad track that runs between thicket hedges. In this somewhat featureless section of the walk, birds often provide the main interest. Thrushes nest in the hedges, and one might hear the tuneful song of the wheatear, a summer visitor from Africa. At the farm buildings, turn right through the wooden gate and at once the nature of the landscape begins to change. The track leads gently uphill to an area of rough grassland patched with gorse that marks the edge of Cleeve Common, the last remaining area of unenclosed wasteland in the Cotswolds. Instead of having paths defined by hedges and walls, stiles and gates, the common is a great open area criss-crossed by a multitude of paths and bridleways. The Cotswold Way is mostly marked quite clearly, but a certain amount of careful attention is needed to keep to the route.

Beyond the gate at the edge of the common, go straight ahead towards the line of white posts. Where the paths cross, at the top of the rise, turn right. Short turf interspersed with tussock-grass and gorse provides ideal walking, and there are views of a steep-sided, wooded valley. The broad grassy track now dips slightly. Where the way divides, turn left towards the white post and then right again through the gorse. At the top of the hill, by the post, turn off the very broad track onto a narrower path running off to the right. This heads down into a valley **B**, the opposite side of which is scarred by quarry and gravel workings. It is a dramatic landscape, but it is worth keeping one's eyes open for delights closer at hand: five species of orchid grow near the edge of the common. The path goes steeply downhill towards a white post, after which the track is followed round the side of the valley, pitted on both sides by quarries. The path keeps to one of the old quarry tracks terraced into the hill. Near the quarry, by a post with two yellow arrows, turn sharply left to go down to the valley floor, and then turn right. Cross over the little stream and continue on to the Washpool **16**. Postlip Hall can be glimpsed up ahead among the trees. At the white post by a stand of large beech trees, turn off the track that goes round the edge of the wood and carry on up the steep hillside. The way ahead is marked by white posts.

It is rather an anticlimax to discover that the wildness has suddenly given way to something as prosaic as a golf course. Continue straight on and, at the second white post, take the path through the gorse, marked by white posts leading towards the clubhouse. Just before this is reached, turn left onto the broad track, then take the further of the two broad tracks. The path now leads to the escarpment edge and Castle Rock **17**, going round the edge to the very impressive ramparts of a hill-fort **18**. All the time, the walker is treated to some

The wildest part of the Way. The arrow points to the faint track over Cleeve Common.

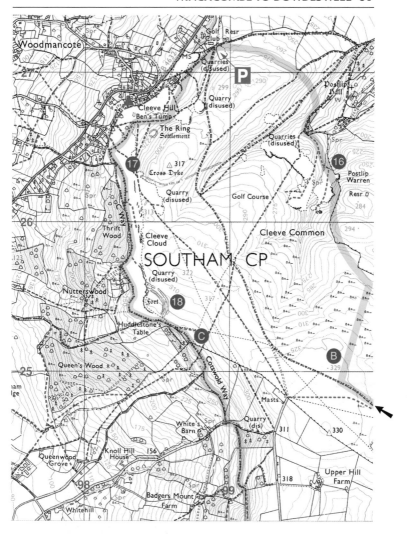

of the best views of the Cotswold Way. Beyond the fort, a seat **C** provides a chance to enjoy the panorama in comfort. The path follows the line of the wall to a notice board by a gate. Go through the gate and follow the bridleway downhill along a wire fence. Now go through the wooden gate and follow the track round to the left, and then round beside the woodland. Beyond the iron gate, continue on the path, which swings to the left. Where the ways meet, continue straight on past a little knoll covered with scrub on the right.

Cleeve Hill has never been farmed and is rich in wild flowers.

The uplands are now very much left behind as the path enters the shelter of Happy Valley **19**, which is rather unhappy in wet weather when the bridleway is churned up by horses' hooves. Even then, however, this is an attractive and peaceful area. At the head of the valley, cross the stile and continue along the track through the gorse to a quarry **D**. Here the path turns down to the right and leads to a stile, after which it turns left round the quarry. The wide track now brings us back to farmland. At the end of the lane, join the roadway and then turn immediately left to follow the path beside the hedge. Turn left again at the road, where beech trees form a processional avenue. At the crossroads turn right and, shortly after passing a barn where the road swings round to the left, turn right over the stile to follow the path along the side of the wall. Cross over the road and go straight on. Where the fence turns to the right, the path continues round the edge of Dowdeswell Wood, planted during the Depression of the 1930s when no one wanted agricultural land. There is now a wide range of conifers here, and in season these are brightened by bluebells and wood anemones. This steep path is almost invariably wet and muddy – it might well prove easier to descend on skis or a tea tray than in walking boots. The problem is largely caused by springs, and there are plans to improve the drainage. The reservoir **20** comes briefly into view on the left. The slither completed, follow the track over the reservoir outflow round to the right to emerge by the water-treatment plant on the busy A40 opposite the Reservoir Inn.

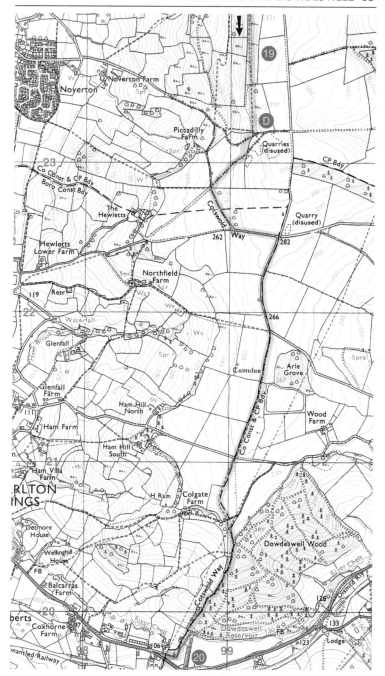

CIRCULAR WALK FROM WINCHCOMBE

4½ miles (7 km)

The walk begins at the gateway **14** to Sudeley Castle. The Cotswold Way turns off to the right, but for this route continue straight on along the main driveway between an avenue of trees. Go over a bridge and, just before the house, turn off to the right by the Footpath sign **A** to follow the path round the side of the house. At first sight, Sudeley Castle looks like a Gothic-revival country mansion, but it is in fact based on an original Norman fortress. Among its most famous inhabitants was Katherine Parr, one of the unfortunate wives of Henry VIII. Lord Chandos held Sudeley during the Civil War and, having supported the Royalists, kept his lands only on condition that the castle was slighted. It fell into neglect until the early nineteenth century when it passed to the Dent family, who restored it – hence its present appearance.

At the gate by the house, continue in the direction indicated by the yellow arrow, going across the open parkland on a slight diagonal to the right, marked by a line of posts. Leave the park by the stile over the stream, turn right, then left to go through the farm gate. Follow the path across the field in the direction of the telegraph pole on the horizon. Continue across the next field, heading towards the right-hand edge of the wood. Cross the stile and follow the path along the side of the woodland. At the end of the wood, cross another stile by a stream and continue over rough grassland. At the farm track, turn left.

Rounding the bend, a loud splashing of water can be heard over to the right. A few yards off the track are the ruined remains of a small mill with its water wheel still in place **21**. Beyond the buildings is a substantial mill pond. The stony track passes through a cluster of barns to emerge on a grassy hill. Shortly before reaching the house at the top, turn left through the gate with the yellow arrow to join the broad track. From here there is a splendid view back down the valley to Winchcombe. Where the broad track swings round to the right, continue straight on towards the gap between the two woods. At the gap, turn left to cross the stile and join the footpath that leads through the wood, going downhill to a clearing. Do not follow the broad track to the left, but turn slightly right to cross the clearing and continue on the narrow path through the trees, arriving at an area of tumbled walls and fallen stones which is all that remains of a Roman villa **22**.

Leave the wood by the stile and turn left to follow the path alongside the wood. Where the path divides by a small stand of conifer, turn right. Cross two stiles and continue past the telegraph pole. Go through the line of conifers by the two stiles, crossing an area of coarse grassland and heading towards the farm buildings opposite. The route now turns left through the gatepost with the arrows to join the broad track, passing a lake created by the damming of a small stream. Where the broad track swings round to the right, continue straight on through the gate and follow the line of the hedge as shown by the footpath sign. At the end of the field, cross the broad track to the stile and head across the park to Sudeley Castle to return to the start.

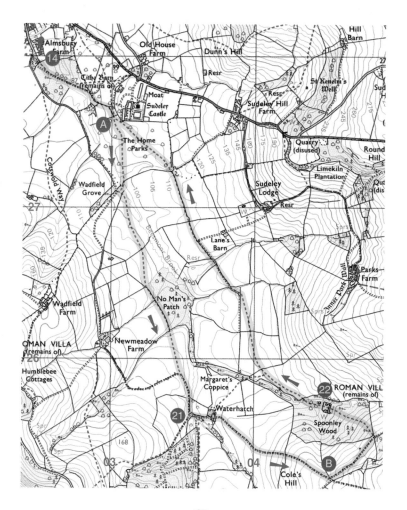

The old banqueting hall at Sudeley Castle still retains something of its former grande

3 DOWDESWELL TO PAINSWICK

via Leckhampton Hill and Cooper's Hill   *17 ½ miles (28 km)*

Turn left at the pavement by the A40 and, where the road bears left, cross over and go straight uphill on the path. Across the stile is the track of the old Great Western Railway branch, linking Cheltenham to the main Oxford line. There are reminders of those days in the metal posts, which are cut down from the distinctive GWR rails. Continue on the path uphill to the dense patch of conifers and take the narrow lane bordered by a thicket hedge, the branches of which meet overhead to create a green tunnel. The path swings round to the left to cut through the narrow neck of woodland **A**. Cross the stile and turn right to follow the line of the fence, then right again over the stile by the wooden gate to take the path through Lineover Wood. A little way along is a tree stump protected by what looks like an overgrown basket, known as a 'dead hedge'. The stump is that of a rare large-leaved lime tree, which has been cut back to allow new shoots to develop. The dead hedge protects the tender growth from deer. The path follows the edge of the woodland to emerge at a stile by an iron gate. Go straight on up the hill towards the wooden post. At the top of the hill, go through the iron gate beneath the power lines and take the narrow footpath beside the fence. Where the fence begins to turn to the right, bear left by the post with the yellow arrow to take the narrow but obvious footpath that climbs diagonally up the hill. At the top of the escarpment go through the iron gate and take the path through the narrow strip of woodland, straight on across the field to the road **B**.

There is now a choice of routes. The shortest involves turning right for a walk of 1 mile (1.5 km) to Seven Springs, following a noisy and busy main road with very little in the way of a verge to offer protection from the traffic. The alternative route is 2½ miles (4 km) long and offers pleasant countryside but, it has to be said, presents something of a quagmire in parts during wet weather. For this route, cross straight over the road and follow the surfaced track that runs beside Chatcombe Wood, leaving the concrete where it swings off to the shooting range, and continuing on the gravel track. The dense conifers soon give way to broad-leaved woodland, carpeted first with bluebells and later by dog mercury. At the wooden gate close to the junction of the power lines **C**, turn diagonally right across the field, heading first for the post by a

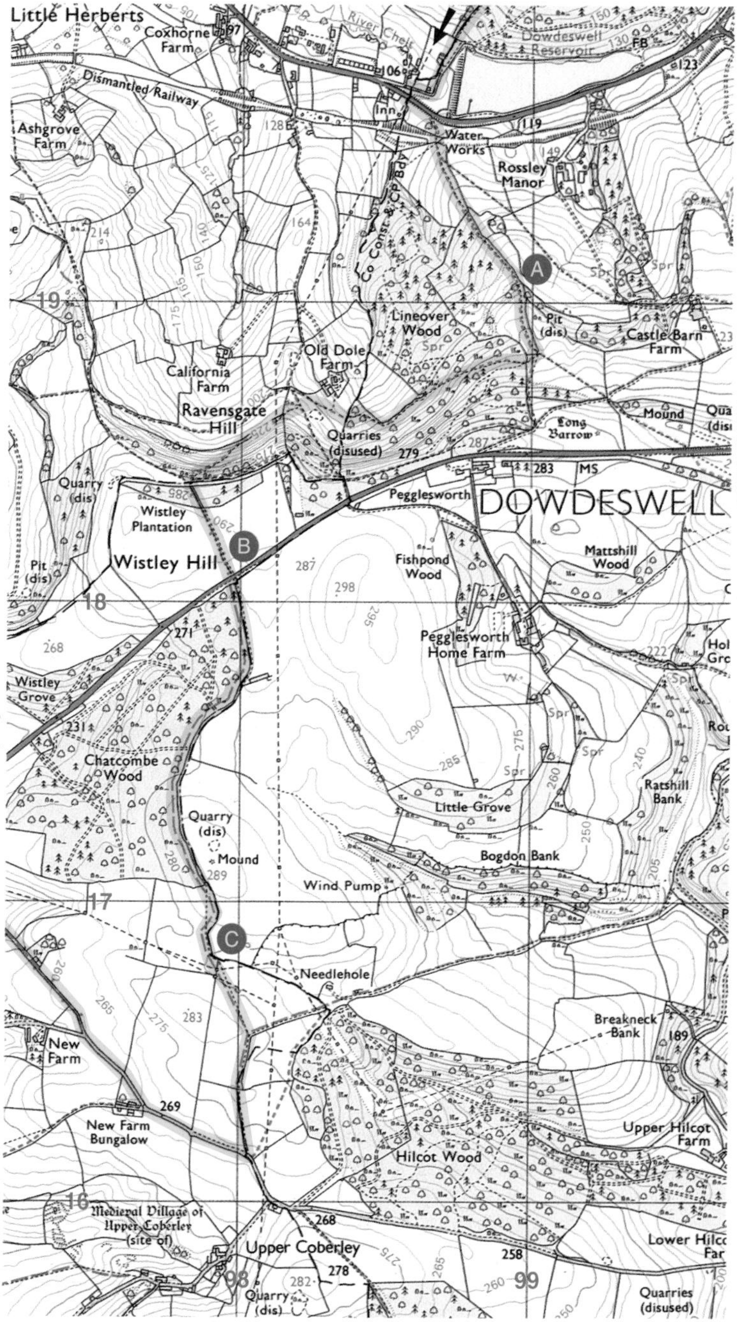

A436 Andoversford
3 km or 2 miles

A36
Seven Springs

clump of trees and then for the white disc beyond that. Turn right onto the bridleway, then right at the road. Where the road swings sharply round to the left, take the broad track to the right which leads down to the main road at Seven Springs **23**. Here the two routes reunite. The Seven Springs themselves are said, on somewhat dubious grounds, to be the source of the Thames; they can be found near Seven Springs House, down the A436 to the left.

Go straight over the crossroads – or for those using the A436, turn right – onto the A435, then turn immediately left onto the minor road. Windmill Farm **24** lives up to its name, still having two (albeit inactive) wind pumps in the fields. Where the road turns left, continue straight on along the path between the fence and the hedge. The way divides by a tangled thicket; turn left here, going uphill, then turn right to follow the line of the hedge. A little path wanders through a patch of woodland to emerge dramatically at the lip of one of the steepest parts of the escarpment. The path stays on the edge of the escarpment, then swings left through a hummocky landscape, spattered with gorse and wind-bent trees. Where the way divides **D** in the little wooded area, turn left to leave the humps and hollows for

The Devil's Chimney, a rocky pinnacle left behind by quarrying on the escarpment at Leckhampton.

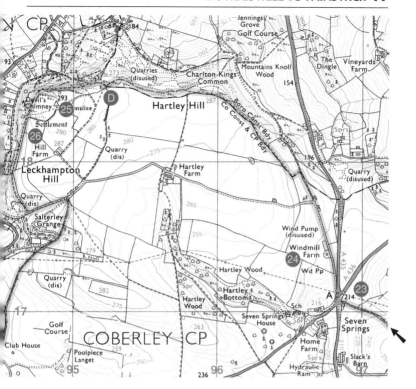

an area of smooth turf. At the top of the hill is a topograph **25**. Since this was put here a new landscape feature has appeared; the two broad white stripes on the hill above Gloucester are artificial ski slopes. The escarpment along this section of the walk has been eaten away by quarries, and there is a multitude of tracks inviting exploration. Below the escarpment edge, the level terraces were used by tramways, i.e. horse-drawn railways. To allow enough space for the horses to walk between them, the rails were mounted on parallel rows of square stone sleepers instead of on the more familiar wooden sleepers. Some of these can still be found *in situ*. The walk now reaches a famous landmark: the tall pillar of rock left behind by the quarrymen and known as The Devil's Chimney **26**.

The path swings steadily round to the left to follow the side of a shallow valley with a road running up the middle. Turn left onto this road and, at the top of the hill, just before reaching the white house, turn right onto a bridleway that runs past Salterley Grange. Continue on past the golf course on the left and turn right onto the road. On the left is the park and ornamental lake of Ullenwood Manor, now a College of Further Education. Beyond the high conifer windbreak, continue straight on at the crossroads through an area of rich pasture, grazed by horses in place of the more familiar sheep. An old army camp has lost its soldiers but gained a considerable army of rabbits. As the road begins to go downhill past the woodland, turn left up the steps and take the path along the bottom edge of the wood. Here the escarpment sweeps round in a graceful curve emphasised by tall trees. Over to the left, through the screen of trees, is a hump bristling with conifers. This is Shurdington Neolithic long barrow **27** – nowhere near as well preserved as Belas Knap. This pleasant walk along the edge gives uninterrupted views over towards Gloucester. By the National Trust signpost for Crickley Hill, cross over the stile to continue on the same path. Do *not* cross the second stile into the woods but continue along the edge of the escarpment beside the wood, where a good deal of new planting is going on. The path emerges at an area of springy turf. Go through the car park and on through the lower car park created out of an old quarry to take the path that leads to the ramparts of the promontory fort **28**, first inhabited at least 5,000 years ago in the New Stone Age. Two ditches were dug and the excavated stone piled up to form ramparts, creating an enclosed camp, inside which archaeologists have found hundreds of stone arrowheads. The site was abandoned somewhere around 2,500 BC and remained forgotten until the seventh century BC, when even stronger defences were built with the prominent deep ditch and high wall that can be seen today. A defended roadway led into the site, which had houses and storage huts. The steep escarpment provided the natural defences around the rest of the promontory. This is one of the earliest known defended sites in Britain, and is well worth exploring.

Leave the promontory by the stile **E** and follow the line of the stone wall. There is a fine view over the great scooped-out hollow of a natural amphitheatre, and the setting would be idyllic but for the noise of traffic on the main road. Indeed, the next objective can be seen up ahead – a large, green roundabout sign. Continue down by the wooden fence, then follow the rather vague track through the wood, waymarked by the occasional yellow arrow on a tree. As the road comes into view, turn right to go through a wooden gate and follow the path beside the road. Turn right immediately beyond the buildings, cross the roundabout and join the pavement along the A417, which keeps to the left of the Air Balloon. Stay on the pavement as it turns away from the road, then bear right to take the path through the woods. The route leads round the hillside opposite Crickley Hill, passing just below the car park, where there are two topographs, one panoramic and one geological **29**. The path follows the boundary between the farmland and the edge of the escarpment. Enter the woodland by the stile and go on to the end of the promontory, where, by a waymark post, the path doubles back on itself **F**. Cross over the road and take the path downhill. At the bottom

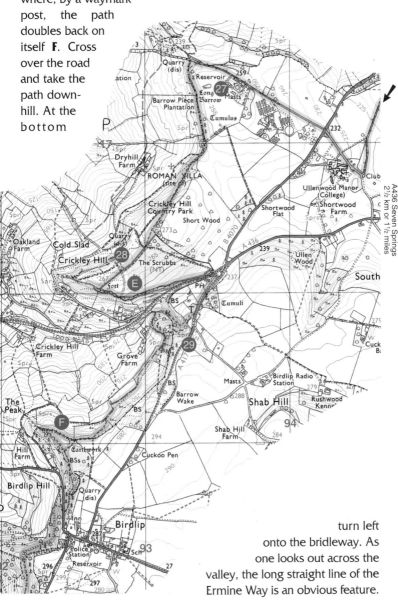

A436 Seven Springs
2½ km or 1½ miles

turn left onto the bridleway. As one looks out across the valley, the long straight line of the Ermine Way is an obvious feature.

Woodland now dominates the walk for several miles, with just the occasional break. Where the track divides, take the route to the left, going uphill. The bridleway now joins a broad forest track. Turn right and follow it downhill, continuing along the same obvious tracks until reaching a T-junction. Turn uphill to the left, where the track runs along beside the old boundary wall marking the edge of Witcombe Park. Just beyond a very grand gateway, the track divides: turn right and right again. A small clearing comes as a relief, for these woods lack the character of some of the beech woods met elsewhere along the way. Where the path divides by a wooden gate, continue straight on; over to the right is the first glimpse of the Roman villa of Great Witcombe **30**, looking like a full-scale architect's drawing spread out on the ground. It resembles a modern farm in its lay-out, with house and outbuildings set around a yard. Where the bridleway turns off to the left, carry straight on. The path crosses a stream trickling down a little valley. Beyond this, take the path up to the left. There is now a better view of the villa, which is not accessible from the walk.

The Way is once again running along the edge of the escarpment; it emerges from the wood at the village of Cooper's Hill and the welcoming sign of the Haven Tea Garden. Looking out from the hillside, the most prominent feature is the busy M5. Turn left by a steep grassy slope to take the path uphill.

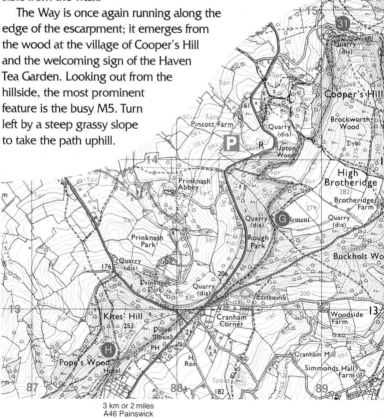

3 km or 2 miles
A46 Painswick

Turn left again to continue climbing the hill until you reach the maypole **31**. This is the site of the annual Whit Monday cheese rolling. The cheese is set bounding off down the hill with locals in pursuit. Turn away from the slope and head past the post with the arrow. The path meanders gently downhill and the way divides at the bottom. Take the far track at the edge of the wood and turn right into a lane bordered by holly. Go through a narrow stile and follow the path round to the left along the upper edge of the wood. The noise of traffic becomes louder and there are glimpses of the A46 twisting up the hill. The woodland was originally coppiced to provide poles for charcoal burning. A number of nature trails thread through the woods, which can make for a little confusion. The Way passes steps on the right and then goes uphill to the left, following the wall to the beginning of a superb beech wood.

The path divides by the notice board saying 'Welcome to Buckholt Wood' **G**. Take the path to the right along the edge of the wood, and go downhill by a broken-down stone wall on the right. As the woods thin out there are views over Prinknash Park. Turn right onto the minor road and follow it down to the A46. Cross over and take the footpath

to the left of the stone wall. In summer the woodland air is heavy with the aroma of wild garlic. Walk past the stone stile in the wall to the right, and then, when the way divides, turn slightly uphill to the left. Cross the minor road and go straight on along the footpath immediately opposite. At the roadway by Castle Lodge **H**, turn right then immediately left to take the broad

Cooper's Hill: the Cotswold Way is out of sight in the depths of the woods that li

…e ridge.

track past the green on the golf course, as indicated by the wooden post. Beyond the prominent group of conifers are the ramparts of the hill-fort on Painswick Beacon. The outline of the fortifications is largely hidden behind a curtain of spruce and pine. At the roadway turn left and, where the road swings round to the left, turn right to take the path immediately to the left of the quarry. This is now home to a splendid array of architectural features, looking rather lonely when divorced from their buildings. Beyond the quarry, take the narrow path terraced into the hillside through an area of mixed woodland. The path emerges from the wood by the golf club. Continue across the grass to go round the right-hand side of the wall surrounding the cemetery **I**. Cross the road and carry on in the same direction, heading for the waymark by the green. At the roadway turn right towards a curious octagonal building. At the road junction turn left into Painswick.

The route passes Gyde's Orphanage, founded by a Victorian businessman, and then carries on down Gloucester Street. The Way takes a slight detour to provide an architectural tour of Painswick – in fact, the town repays an even longer look. Like so many in the region, it grew wealthy on wool, and the wealth shows. The official route goes straight across the main street into Bisley Street, then right down St Mary's Street to the churchyard. Along the way are a number of fine houses, including Tudor Byfield House. Its arched doorway is an old 'donkey door', which allowed pack animals into the wool barn at the back. But the route misses out Painswick's oddest house, the post office on the main road. This looks like two tiny buildings stuck together, one timber-framed, the other of stone, holding each other up like a pair of drunks as they lean at odd angles. Painswick's chief claim to fame is the churchyard **32**. At the entrance are the village stocks, an oddity in that the miscreants' legs were held in iron hoops. The churchyard contains perhaps the finest set of carved tombs in Britain, around which are a hundred yews. The church, which would be memorable elsewhere, seems almost disappointing in such a setting. It does, however, have its own oddity – a massive model of Drake's flagship, the *Bonaventure*. Adjoining Victoria Square is the start of the circular walk described below.

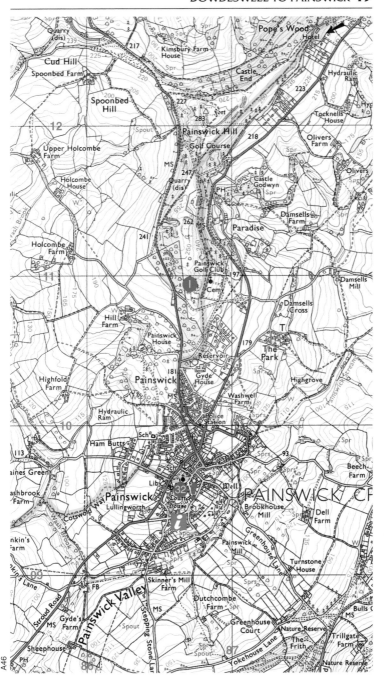

Circular walk from Painswick

5 miles (8 km)

The walk starts at Victoria Square **A** in Painswick next to the church. Leave the main road, passing between the town hall and the churchyard, then turn left into St Mary's Street and right at The Cross. The road goes steeply downhill along Tibwell Lane. A small stream emerges from a conduit at Tebetha's Well to run down the side of the street. At the bottom of the hill is an old mill complex **33**, now converted to housing; the sluice gates that controlled the water for the wheel can be seen on the left. Cross the stream and turn left to follow the track alongside the water. Where the driveway swings round to the right, continue along the quiet path beside the stream, now overhung by trees. The path turns slightly uphill to a stile and then continues by the hedge. On the left is a grand house **34**, which was originally Loveday's cloth mill.

Cross the stile by the house and turn right along the green path that leads uphill. Looking back from this part of the walk, there is a fine view of Painswick and its dominant church. At the farm buildings, turn right onto the broad track and, where this swings round to the left towards the house, continue straight on to the appropriately named village of Longridge. At the roadway turn left and, where the road divides, carry straight on. As the road swings round to the left **B**, take the rough road that runs along the edge of the wood, then continue on the bridleway into Blackstable Wood, part of the Cotswold Commons and Beechwoods National Nature Reserve. The beech themselves rear up beyond an area of turf and clay grassland dotted with young trees, notably silver birch. Where the track divides, go straight on along the bridleway. At the end of the wood, continue past the white house to join the road and turn right.

This is Jack's Green, at the edge of Sheepscombe. On the left is Sheepscombe House, a very grand eighteenth-century building. Where the road divides by the bus shelter, turn left to the village. The lane goes downhill, bordered by a massive beech hedge. A building appears to the right with 'weavers' windows' on the top storey; this was once a loom shop, where cloth was woven. The road passes the church with its small onion dome. Follow the sign for Painswick, noting the 1914–18 war memorial, which has a sundial built into the cross. Continue past the Grange and the Butcher's Arms **C**.

Immediately beyond the pub, turn right up the steep lane, sign-posted 'Bridleway', towards the woodland. At the top of the hill follow the footpath round to the left past an area of broken ground marking an old quarry. The path goes through a little copse then crosses a stone stile to enter Lords and Ladies Wood. Follow the obvious route that climbs steadily uphill. Near the top of the hill, the path divides by a tree marked with two yellow arrows; follow the path round to the left. It is not very distinct, but keeps more or less to the edge of the woodland.

Leave the wood at the stile, and continue on, following the line of the fence. Go through the wooden gate into the tree-lined lane that leads past the house to the road. Continue straight on across the road to take the lane opposite, bordered by a hawthorn hedge. At Painswick Lodge, the public right of way has been diverted. Turn left at the road **D**, past the cottages, then turn right by the footpath sign and continue along the side of the field to the next stile, beyond which the path is waymarked by yellow arrows on posts. The walk then follows the line of the stream through a little wooded valley, which gets very muddy in wet weather. At the stile at the end of the wood, turn right in the direction indicated by the yellow arrow. On reaching the next gate, follow the Public Footpath sign at the side of the hedge. Cross two stiles to go along the opposite side of the hedge. Cross the stile by the house and continue on the broad track. Where the track swings round to the right, carry straight on over the stile and across the field. At the stile by the stream, head for another stile just to the right of the conifers at the top of the hill. Cross this and turn left, then right at the roadway. The road winds up to the main road at Painswick. Turn left to return to the start.

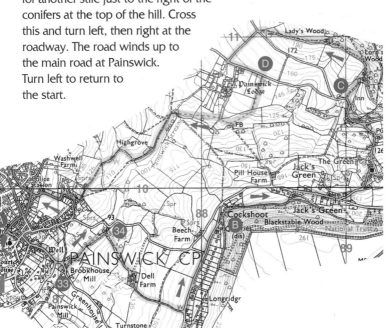

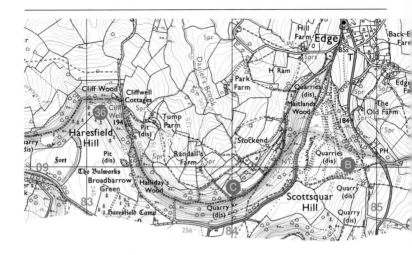

4 PAINSWICK TO ULEY BURY

via Haresfield Beacon and Stanley Mill   *12 ½ miles (20 km)*

Leave the churchyard by the lych gate **A**, cross the main road and take Edge Road out of Painswick. A view now opens up across the Frome valley to the receding line of the escarpment. Just beyond the house with yews that almost match those of the churchyard, turn left through the kissing gate to follow the path alongside the hedge. This small field is being preserved as a traditional meadow. Cross the stile to take the very narrow lane between hedges, then turn immediately left onto an equally narrow path down beside the driveway of a house. Once in the open, follow the line of the fence and then the hedge. At the edge of the rugby field, turn diagonally right towards the white disc. At the disc continue following the line of the hedge.

The Way runs past Washbrook Farm **35**, which has a beautiful doorway with a carved coat of arms, dated 1691. Over the years, the house has also been used as a mill, both for fulling cloth and grinding grain. Beyond the farm, cross over the roadway and turn left. Follow the track round past the corrugated building; looking back, one can see how Washbrook Farm rises three full storeys. The stony track climbs gently uphill above the meandering Wash Brook. Cross the stile on the left and walk on to the stile by the stream. Someone has thoughtfully provided a seat in this tranquil shaded valley, where the only harsh note is supplied by the local jays. Go on into the little bluebell wood, cross over the footbridge, climb the wooden steps and turn left. This part of the route crosses a field dotted

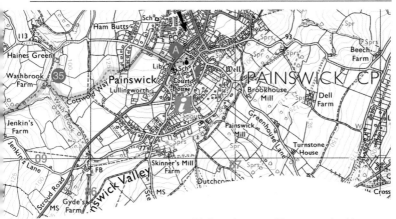

with hawthorn and is waymarked by
wooden posts. The path follows the line of the stream.
Cross the broad farm track and the stile and turn left along the fence and
hedge. Behind you is a good view of Painswick and its tall church spire.

Go through the narrow stile in the stone wall and turn right up the
shady lane. Cross the main road and take the narrow footpath opposite. At the top of the little hill, where the track divides **B**, turn right.
The path goes round the edge of a wood, which is dominated by silver birch. After a little way, leave the track by a post with a yellow
arrow and take the narrow path uphill, waymarked by a line of posts.
The tussock grass is laced with old quarry tracks and paths and is
home to a variety of orchids – six different species have been seen
here. The route goes through the first of the quarries. Just before the
brow of the hill, turn left towards the exposed rock face, then downhill by the steep track with the iron railings, to reach the steps up to
the road. Cross straight over and take the path through the woods,
heading diagonally down across the face of the hill. At the bottom,
where the view opens out across the plain, the broad track becomes
a surfaced road, a quiet lane running along the edge of the woods.
Where this swings away, continue along the bridleway at the foot of
the woods. The path now leads into the trees, waymarked by a blue
arrow with a white dot **C**. Emerging from the wood, continue along
the road past the old quarry workings.

At the cottages, just before the road goes downhill, turn left up the
track towards Cliff Well **36**. This is yet another attractive section where
the pathway runs along the flank of the hillside, overshadowed by tall
beech trees. The same donor who placed the inscription on the well
has also provided a stone seat, the Cromwell Stone, where travellers
can pause and admire the view. Continue to the roadway, turning left

Cowslips cluster on the edge of the promontory of Haresfield Beacon overlooking the Vale of Gloucester.

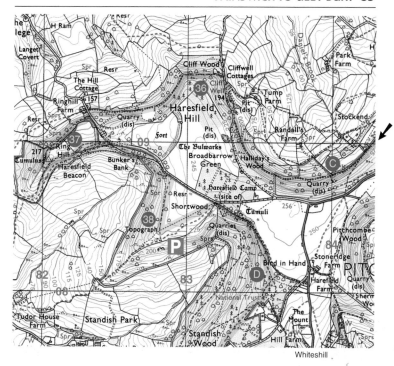

Whiteshill

then right over the stile. At the iron gate by the barn, continue uphill, following the path between the edge of the escarpment and the fence. Crossing a stile, one arrives at an open, grassy promontory, Haresfield Beacon **37**. The view stretches from the towers of Gloucester Cathedral all the way down the Severn valley. Leave the promontory on the opposite, southern side, crossing a stile and following a path between the escarpment edge and the fence. The narrow path keeps to the contours, turns right onto steps going steeply downhill, then follows a stone wall before climbing back uphill to another grassy promontory. At the start of the grassland take the path off to the right to the topograph **38**. From here turn back along the other side of the triangular promontory. Cross the car park, go over the stile and enter Standish Wood by the uppermost of the three tracks.

This is a typical beechwood hanger, with occasional breaks in the trees providing a view down a scooped-out valley. Where several paths meet **D**, continue along the track that bears round to the right. Much of the woodland is newly planted, with the floor carpeted by bluebells and wood anemones. The route keeps to the main, broad track, which is generally well marked by yellow arrows with white dots.

Spinning woollen threads with 'mules' at Stanley Mill.

Beyond the stile and wooden gate, take the path round to the right, which now becomes a bridleway and inevitably somewhat muddier. Where the path divides, turn left and then right onto a broad track that turns into an old roadway running between stone walls. The woodland is now deeply scarred by pits and quarries. The path emerges to give a view across to Stroud on the left and to the Severn valley on the right. One of the most prominent landmarks is the surprisingly elegant stone mill at Ebley, now converted to council offices. Follow the line of the stone wall through a bramble clump and, where it opens out, head left down the field towards the stone stile by a wood. Take the obvious path through the wood, turn left at the lane and then immediately right across a stile. Go down to the path between the houses, and turn right at the road. Turn left opposite a row of cottages set back at an angle to the road, and head off downhill across the fields. Before the iron gate by the massive oak tree, turn right to follow the line of the hedge and continue on towards the obvious tall chimney of Stanley Mill. The path goes above an area of tangled woodland to cross the railway line from Gloucester to Stroud on a footbridge. Continue on the path by the side of the playing field to the main road.

In contrast to the secluded walk through the woods and over high promontories, the Way has now reached the valley floor, with its busy road. Turn right at the road, then left at the mini-roundabout. Here are three generations of transport systems. Having left the road, one crosses the Stroudwater Canal **39**, which linked the Severn to the Thames and Severn Canal, and thus to the Thames itself. Restoration work is moving slowly but steadily ahead. This is followed by the old branch line from Stroud and Nailsworth, converted to a cycle track, but now overtaken by the roadworks of the Ebley bypass. The road runs past the entrance to the Stanley woollen mills **40**, and it is worth peeping in through the gates. Like Ebley, this is a mill with architectural pretensions. Built, rather surprisingly, in brick instead of stone, its façade boasts an array of elegant Venetian windows. Beyond can be seen the mill leat and the sluices that once

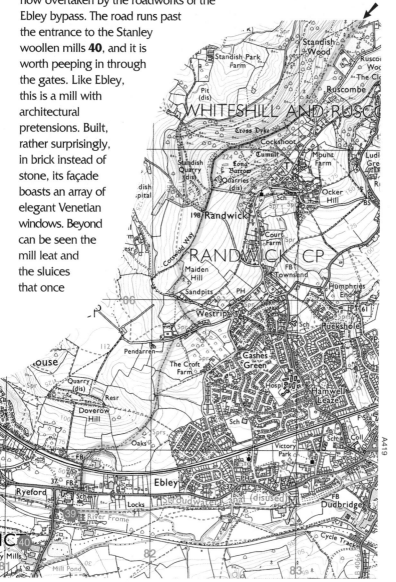

controlled the flow of water to the wheels. Crossing the bridge, turn left onto the track and right over the stile to take the path beside the fence that runs behind the houses. At the stile before the farm buildings, take the upper track running round by the fence. On reaching a group of derelict sheds, follow the path to the left beyond the farm. Cross the roadway and take the path on the diagonal across the arable field, continuing on the same line to the houses of Middleyard on the ridge.

Turn left at the road, then right up Coombe Lane. Where the surfaced road swings away to the left, continue uphill on the track.

Stanley Mill was once water-powered and was among the last working woollen mills in the region.

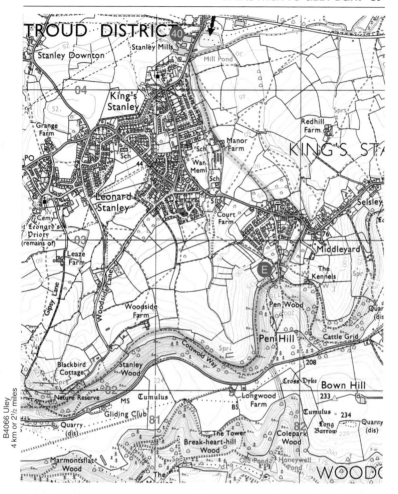

B4066 Uley
4 km or 2½ miles

Emerging from the lane, cut across the field to the stile in the corner
by the house. Turn left at the roadway and immediately left again to
take the stony footpath going steeply uphill **E**. At the top of the hill,
turn right to follow the edge of the woodland. This is another of those
paths that seem to typify this part of the walk, running on a narrow
ledge with mature beech trees to one side and views across the valley to the other. The path stays clear of the woods for a time, crossing
a hollow way and continuing up the wooden steps before approach-
ing the road and swerving away again. Just before the old quarry
workings, turn left up the wooden steps and follow the path along the

Hetty Pegler's Tump. This beautifully preserved long barrow can be reached by a short diversion from the Cotswold Way.

boundary fence to emerge by a car park. Go straight across the road and take the path opposite, which goes past the Nympsfield long barrow **41**, restored in 1976. This is almost as grand as Belas Knap; when excavated, it was found to contain a large quantity of pig bones, as well as human remains. Researchers also discovered that the New Stone Age people had been in need of dental care, suffering from rotting teeth, abscesses and swollen gums.

The path runs round the edge of the steep escarpment slope. The grassy area is popular not just with strollers and picnickers but also with hang gliders. The Way keeps to the edge, squeezed into the area between two roads, and passes more disused quarries. Go down the wooden steps, turn left at the roadway, where there is a handsome cast-iron milestone of a type once common on all the local roads. Immediately before joining the main road, turn right onto the path going down through the woods. Where this divides, take the path to the left. Leave the bridleway – with some relief in wet weather – and follow the footpath up to the left. This is another very attractive woodland walk, but of a different character. There are still beech in plenty, but mixed now with ash and hazel coppices. In the denser, darker woodland flourishes hart's tongue fern. The views, when they appear, are of smoothly rounded hills separated from the escarpment, which is pitted with quarries. At the top of the hill, the Cotswold Way arrives at the high ramparts of Uley Bury hill-fort **42**. This is perhaps the grandest of all the Iron Age forts met en route, enclosing a huge plateau of 13 hectares with double banks and ditches. Those who want to explore the fort can take the mile-long circuit, which is rewarded with tremendous views, or incorporate this into the circular walk that passes this point (see p. 92). The main path, however, now leads downhill to the right.

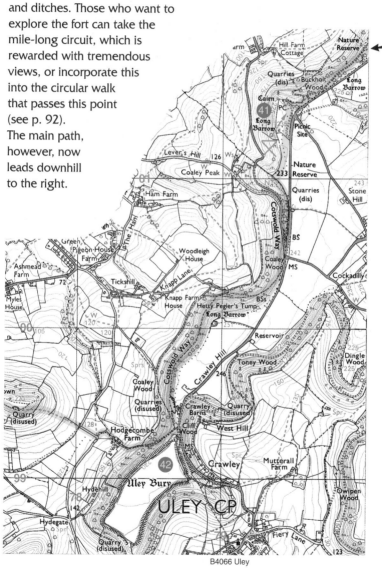

B4066 Uley

Circular walk from Uley Bury

4 miles (6 km)

The walk begins at the point **A** where the Cotswold Way meets the north-west corner of the Uley Bury hill-fort. Take the path up to the top of the ramparts, turn left and left again to follow the edge of the defences. The fort was built in the Iron Age, almost certainly by the local Dobunni tribe. It is protected by two banks and ditches, which enclose a 13-hectare rectangle. At the next corner of the fort **B**, take the path that runs very steeply downhill towards Uley. Cross the stile at the bottom of the woods, follow the path to the houses, go over another stile into the street, and turn right. At the chapel turn left down the hill past Combe House and carry on down to the crossroads where the Bath and Stroud roads intersect. Beyond the house with the ornate wrought-iron porch, continue straight on up the hill. Down to the left is a small stream with a large duck population. Over to the right is Stouts Hill, with its castellations and Gothic windows.

Opposite the green gate and letter box (in the wall on the right), turn left across the stile, then cross the field, heading for the stile immediately to the left of the line of trees. Continue along the hedge to an unusual stile made of old railway sleepers. Once past the farm buildings, cross two stiles, then instead of continuing straight on to the metal gate, turn diagonally to the right to reach the stile in the corner of the field, then go straight uphill towards the woodland. Looking back, the outline of the ramparts of Uley Bury hill-fort can be clearly seen. Cross the stile and continue on up the broad bridleway through the woods, where silver birch provide flashes of light among the darker trees.

At the road turn left to go downhill between high, wooded banks towards the hamlet of Owlpen. The road provides a good view of the Tudor manor house **43**, which is open to the public on some summer days. Alongside is the little church of the Holy Cross, rebuilt in the nineteenth century, and later enriched by mosaics and paintings. The baptistry is very Art Nouveau while the chancel gleams with Byzantine gold patterns under a painted roof.

After visiting the church, continue on the road up the hill. Down in the valley is the distinctive triangular shape of a mill pond. As the road swings downhill to the left, turn right by the yellow arrow on the telegraph pole. Continue through the gate onto the broad track to go up a narrow valley crowned with broad-leaved woodland. Where the track divides by a wooden shed, continue straight on. At the end of the valley **C**, where the telegraph poles turn left, turn back diagonally across the field to a stile in the far corner. Turn right to cross the stream by a clump of trees and continue on towards the farm buildings. Join the broad track that goes round the farm towards the cottage. Immediately before the cottage, turn right to cross the stile tucked away between the garage and the house. Turn left towards the houses. Join the main road, cross over and walk up the hill. After forty yards, turn left up the bridlepath. The path comes out by the ramparts. Turn right to return to the start.

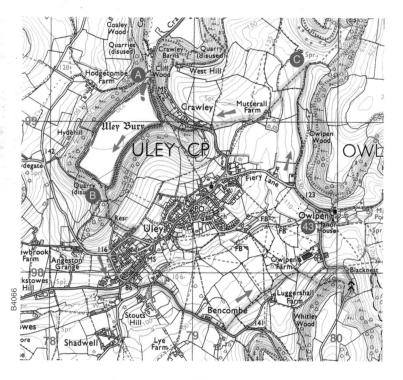

B4066

Owlpen Manor is basically fifteenth century, though altered and enlarged over th

xt three centuries. It was restored by Norman Jewson.

5 ULEY BURY TO WOTTON-UNDER-EDGE

via Cam Long Down and North Nibley 9 ½ miles (15 km)

This may seem like a short, easy section of the walk, but do not be deceived. It takes the prize for strenuous climbs and, as the walker soon discovers, even the downhill sections have their own problems. The path does indeed lead immediately downhill, and one can see at once just how formidable the fort's defences were: the steepness of the slope alone would have made attack difficult. The hill presents an equally daunting obstacle to walkers. The narrow bridleway sunk between tree-topped banks provides natural drainage for the hill and is something of a quagmire in even the driest season. It emerges by a farm with a large pond and a noisy population of ducks and geese. Continue on past the lake towards the rounded hump of Cam Long Down. At the road turn right, and, where the road goes to the right **A**, carry on along the path by the hedge and head straight for the top of the hill.

A flight of wooden steps leads up to the tree-fringed summit and an exhilarating walk along the airy ridge. This is one of the few places on the Way to offer an uninterrupted 360° view, which includes a great length of the escarpment. The summit is full of the humps and hollows of old quarries, and the route goes off along the spine, with turf underfoot – a more than adequate reward for the muddy slide downhill followed by a hard slog up again. At an area of scrub, the path heads downhill to the saddle

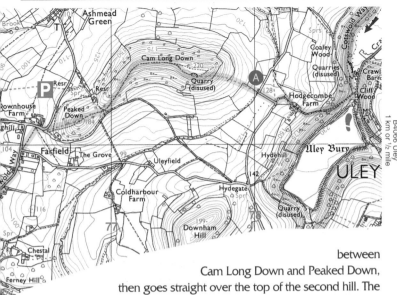

between
Cam Long Down and Peaked Down,
then goes straight over the top of the second hill. The
tower up ahead is a forthcoming, somewhat daunting objective.
Take the broad grassy track down to the road, cross over and continue on the narrow path through the woods. At the roadway turn left
and then left again over a stile by an iron gate. Continue across the fields
via the obvious stiles. At the road junction, go straight on along the road
signposted to Dursley. Just beyond the house with a fine display of ornamental trees, turn left over the stile. At the next stile turn right and continue on across the line of stiles. At the farm buildings, head for the telegraph pole by the red brick house. Go down the steps, through a little
wood, past a bowling green with a rather dainty pavilion, and then past
a terrace of houses to enter the outskirts of Dursley by a small factory.
Turn left up the street, passing the house of Mikael Pederson, who at the
turn of the century invented a bicycle with a geometric frame, and later
developed three-speed gears. At the end of the street is the Market Hall
44, built in 1783, from which a rather crude statue of Queen Anne peers
across at the church. The latter was largely rebuilt in the fourteenth century, and once had a spire, which collapsed in 1698.

Cross the road by the Market House and go up the pedestrianised
street. Turn left into May Lane then right past the Old Spot Inn and
take the road that goes steeply uphill. As the road turns left, go
straight on along the broad track and, where this forks, take the path
on the left uphill through the woods to arrive eventually at a clubhouse
by a golf course. Here, there is something of a multiplicity of routes on
offer. Stinchcombe Hill is an unevenly shaped plateau, with constantly

Cam Long Down, thrusting out into the plain, with the River Severn and the

Tyndale Monument just visible in the distance.

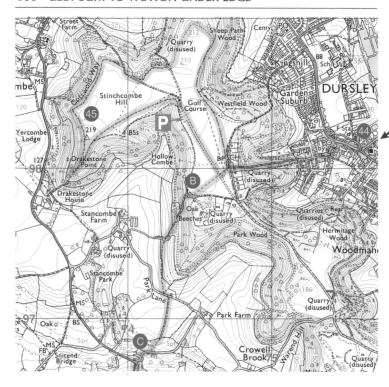

changing views from its edge. Leave the plateau by a downhill path, a couple of hundred yards away to the left **B**. The official route provides a 2 mile (3 km) circular trip around most of the edge, but having come this far, one might wish to extend the walk to a complete (2 ½ mile) circuit. For those enthusiasts, the following description covers the whole circuit. Being virtually a circular route it matters little which way one goes, but it is marginally easier clockwise.

Starting from the clubhouse, follow the road from the car park across the golf course and, where that ends, take the path to the left round the rim (the view includes the monument and the Severn Bridge). The route dips down through scrub and, at the end of the promontory, climbs up again to the trig point, past an ornamental stone seat. Now the view extends to the distant cranes and warehouses of Sharpness. The path runs along the edge, past a topograph, just below the tip of the escarpment, and comes to a shelter with an attractive weather vane showing a plus-foured golfer trying to hit his way out of a bunker **45**. Continue on round the edge and turn right to return to the golf course. A track now leads to the car park at the end of the road, and back to the clubhouse and the Cotswold Way. For the full circuit continue on the bridleway round the edge of the course.

On leaving the clubhouse, walk across the roadway to the stone wall. Follow the road round to the right and, just beyond the end of the wall, turn left onto the track that plunges down through the woods, which are notable for a number of massive beech trees. Where the track comes out into the open, turn left off the bridleway onto a footpath. Cross the stile and follow the line of the fence, taking the obvious path through the fields and over stiles. The next objective, North Nibley, can be seen on the hillside opposite. At the roadway turn left and then follow the footpath, heading in a straight line across the field. At the far side, head for the wooden post, then turn diagonally right at the stile. Turn right at the road **C** and cross the stream by the mill and mill pond, then take the lane, bordered by trees, that goes uphill to North Nibley. At the top of what turns out to be yet another steep

The monument erected to the memory of the martyr William Tyndale, who translated the Bible into English.

track, turn left at the triangular green and follow the road down to the junction and the Black Horse Inn – a very welcome sight after so many hills. This peaceful village has a surprisingly bloody history. In 1470 battle was joined over the ownership of the vast Berkeley estates, and an estimated 150 men died, including the young Lord Lisle. The military action settled nothing and centuries of legal action followed.

Suitably refreshed, walkers now follow the main road towards Wotton-under-Edge for a short way. The promise of an easy stroll is short lived. Just past the old milestone, the Way turns left to continue resolutely up the face of the hill. A little further along, turn right onto the wooden steps for an even more direct ascent. A splendid gnarled old beech spreads its branches over the path, as if providing a ceremonial entrance to the Tyndale Monument **46**. This was erected in memory of William Tyndale, who translated the Bible into English, an action which found no favour with the Church. Tyndale died at the stake, martyred in 1536.

From the monument follow the edge of the escarpment past the topograph, set in a large boulder. The path follows the boundary fence and, looking ahead, one begins to get a sense that the Cotswolds will soon be coming to an end. Instead of a steep scarp that seems to stretch to the horizon, there is an altogether gentler swell of hills to the south, and a widening plain. For the moment, however, a familiar pattern is resumed, as the path enters the beech wood. Beyond the gate take the wide track swinging round to the right. At the junction of many ways **D**, continue on the same line and, at the next division of the track, turn to the left, waymarked by a blue arrow and white dot. To the right are the bank and ditch of Brackenbury hill-fort **47**, while to the left is a typical dense, modern conifer plantation. This is pleasant, easy walking and a screen of broad-leaved trees, mainly beech, provides some light amid the tightly packed larch. Occasional openings in the trees give good views to the right. As the woodland comes to an end on the left, turn right beside the wide expanse of arable fields. Emerging from the woods, take the path between the field and the woods. At the end of the field cross the stile and begin to head downhill past a stand of conifers **48**. The trees were originally planted in 1815 to commemorate the battle of Waterloo and have been renewed twice since then. From here, take the path that winds its way through the scrub and brambles heading down to Wotton-under-Edge. Cross a stile and continue on the footpath opposite. This eventually becomes a paved track leading down to the road. At the road continue in the same direction and, where the road divides before the garage, turn right to reach the centre of the town.

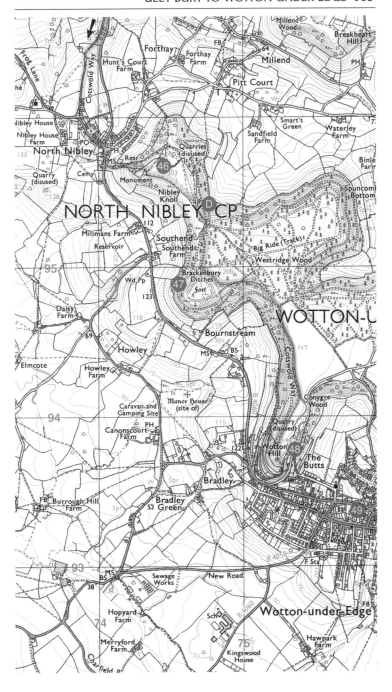

Wotton-under-Edge is yet another wool town, and the mills were once found right in the centre. The steam-powered Old Town Mill, for example, is now a Catholic church. As elsewhere, the wealth generated was often put to charitable use, and produced some of the town's finest buildings. The Cotswold Way follows a somewhat circuitous route, but still takes in much that is worth seeing. Go down Bradley Street to High Street and Long Street, overlooked by an ornate Jubilee clock. Turn left into Church Street, graced by the Perry and Dawes Almshouses **49**. These are an absolute gem. First endowed by Hugh Perry (or Perii, as the original inscription has it) in 1638, they represent Cotswold domestic architecture at its best. Just look, for example, at the roof with its neat cupola and range of gables. A simple chapel was built in the courtyard, and is lit by a stained-glass window showing sheep and wool spinners.

Once past the almshouses, cross over the road at the junction and take the high-level footpath that curves away from the road. Go down Shinbone Alley, between the houses and the wall. Turn left to enter the churchyard. Here is yet another of those splendid Cotswold churches with a noble tower. The interior has a great feeling of spaciousness and only after taking in the splendour of the whole design does one notice the many enchanting details. Pride of place has to go to two fourteenth-century monumental brasses depicting Lord and Lady Berkeley. Lord Berkeley's armour features a collar decorated with mermaids. Having looked down, look up at the ceiling bosses, which show the medieval carver's penchant for the grotesque.

Continuing through the churchyard, turn right at the road. Opposite is another row of almshouses, now rather overwhelmed by new development. Turn right down Valley Road and follow it round to the left to leave the town.

The Perry and Dawes Almshouses at Wotton-under-Edge. Behind the façade is a charming courtyard and tiny chapel.

6 WOTTON-UNDER-EDGE TO TORMARTON

via Horton   *14 miles (22.5 km)*

The road out of Wotton-under-Edge is accompanied by a fast-flowing stream. When the houses are left behind, this becomes a very pleasant stroll, with a hedge which is home to numerous birds on one side, and the stream with its water plants, including golden saxifrage, water forget-me-not and yellow flag, on the other. The path passes the hamlet of Holywell **A** and goes through a dogleg before continuing beside the stream. Over to the left on Coombe Hill is a very prominent set of lynchets **50**, marking the site of medieval strip fields. Faced by the steep hillside, the farmers of the day created a series of broad ledges, similar to the cultivation terraces used in many mountainous areas of the world. At the roadway at Coombe, turn right. The stream has been dammed, originally to feed the mills.

After the houses, turn left off the road and immediately right into a little lane beneath an overhanging hedge. Looking back one can see the reservoir whose outflow keeps the stream so busy. Near the top of the hill, the path begins to zigzag, which eases the ascent. A few harebells cling to the banks before the path enters a narrow strip of woodland, home to a large, clamorous rookery. At the road turn left; here one is back in upland farming country with large, flat fields divided off by low walls and hedges. Down to the left, attractive valleys strike off at right angles to the escarpment. The hills swell up on either side, marked here and there by more strip lynchets and by patches of woodland which curve with the land.

A wood now appears to the left of the road. Just beyond this, take the track on the right that turns sharply back from the road. The hump in the field on the left is another long barrow, completely covered over. This spot provides one of the best views back over the valley. The mixture of field, hedgerow and woodland seems to suit the partridge; these birds are often heard here, and occasionally seen as dumpy figures waddling across a field. Where the track swings to the left, continue straight on through the wooden gate to take the path round the promontory. As always, arrival at the edge brings wide vistas, this time over to the Mendips and the more distant Quantocks. Follow the rim of the escarpment above a hollow.

Cross the stile to enter the wood and take the obvious path through the coppices. Climb up a short hill with the help of steps and turn right onto the broad farm track and bridle-way. Go down through a conifer plantation, continuing on the obvious track. At a large clearing **B**, turn off the wide track to take the footpath heading more steeply downhill. This path runs as a hollow way beside an old woodland boundary. The ground here is of sand and soft clay, which has been worn right down to the bedrock. In spring the slopes and banks are bright with wood violets and primroses. As the path descends, so the banks on either side get higher and gloomier, and the flowers give way to the dark green of hart's tongue fern. Erosion has eaten around the roots of trees, and one earth fall has taken an entire mature beech down the slope with it. As the path opens out at the bottom, the flowers return with the addition of masses of celandine.

The hollow way runs right down to the valley floor by a farm. Cross the stile, turn left and cross straight over the road. Turn diagonally to the left and head for the stile visible in the hedge. Cross the next stile and continue towards the telegraph pole. Here there is an impressive old barn with a handsome wagon porch, while over to the left is a small reservoir and pumping station **51**. Originally, and not surprisingly, this was a mill site, known as Monk's Mill, described in 1612 as 'fullinge milles and gryste milles or corn milles'. Cross one stile by a large oak tree and another by an iron gate. Cross over the stream and turn right onto the bridleway. Turn right again at the road into Alderley **52**, which consists largely of a single street of cottages, including a row with a parade of dormer windows under stone-tile covering. The Elizabethan mansion, now a school, seems all but overwhelmed by chimneys, while the nearby church, which was largely rebuilt in the early nineteenth century, is mainly notable for a *trompe-l'oeil* ceiling, painted to represent fan vaulting. The Way now passes by an elegant eighteenth-century Cotswold house with a stone roof and dormers lurking behind the parpet. The grand gateway opposite provides a view up to a folly tower on the hill.

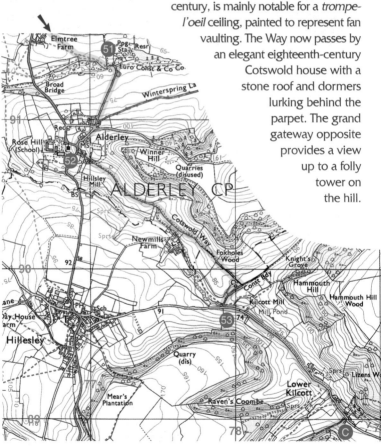

The rare but welcome sight of a field of poppies.

One senses a definite change in the landscape. The escarpment is still there, but the edge is no longer quite so clearly defined. The curves of the hills seem gentler. The path runs beside a wire fence and, down below, one can see a considerable fall of water, marking the site of Hillsley Mill. To the left are the remains of more strip lynchets. The path keeps mainly to the fence, occasionally ducking through small thickets. Newmills Farm, just below the level of the path, was a new mill back in 1636, and it was here in 1806 that some of the first power looms of the region were installed. Carry on along the lane bordered by hedges, which turns out to be a well-churned bridleway. At the end of this track turn right, noting the now sadly rare sight of a properly layered hedge, where the branches are trained to grow horizontally and not simply ripped into shape by a mechanical cutter. The stony lane leads to a stream falling over rocky ledges. Turn left at the road and cross the second stream. Yet again a rush of water announces the presence of a weir and thus a mill **53**. It is hard to believe that this peaceful valley once represented serious competition to the industries of Yorkshire and Lancashire, but it did. Memories also survive in names; the field beside the road is Rack Close, a reminder of when cloth was hung up to dry. The mill pond has silted up, allowing reeds to develop. This very pleasant country lane follows the line of the Kilcott Brook, where moorhen and mallard drift effortlessly with the stream, in the shade of willow. Lower Kilcott now appears and a second mill with it. Turn right up a sunken lane **C** by the group of houses.

The dry surface of the road is exchanged for the wet mud of a bridleway. Where the track divides, carry straight on uphill through the iron gate. Here is a quintessentially English landscape of pasture, arable and woods, which two centuries ago must have looked much as it does now. There is even that rare survivor from disease, a majestic elm. At the end of the field take the stile on the left and follow the footpath as it winds uphill through a tangle of trees dripping with old man's beard. At the bridleway turn left and continue on along the footpath between the hedges. Leaving the woodland behind, head out across the field roughly in the direction of the farm buildings. The top of the Somerset Monument **54** suddenly pops into view above the brow of the hill. Turn left onto what is quite a busy road leading up to the monument. Architecturally this is something of an oddity, the carving at the top looking as if it might be more at home on a pagoda. General Lord Somerset's claim to fame has nothing oriental about it, however – he served at Waterloo.

Continue along the road past the monument towards Hawkesbury Upton. Turn right just before the duck pond and then left onto the bridleway by the small stone building. This is a broad, stony track running between hedges, which supports an active bird community; the song of the blackbird forms an almost continuous accompaniment to the walk. Footpaths to the left can be used for a short diversion to Hawkesbury Upton, where there are two pubs. Just before the roadway, turn left to follow the path by the hedge. Go over two stiles and then turn diagonally right, heading towards the small pond surrounded by trees **D**. The path runs along the side of a hollow, which is not always the most peaceful spot on the walk, as it is used as a motorcycle scrambling course. The route, waymarked by yellow arrows with white dots, eventually heads downhill to the stile at the edge of the wood. Cross this stile and take the path through the woods round to the left. These woods, largely of beech and horse chestnut, are notable for their numerous toadstools. The path twists and turns through the trees, then turns sharply downhill to the right to leave the wood. The Tyndale Monument now appears in the distance.

The route passes Horton Court **55**, at the heart of which is a single-storey Norman hall house, home to the prebendary of the adjoining church. The typical Cotswold manor was built alongside, and in the gardens is a charming Italianate loggia of the sixteenth century – altogether an extraordinary range of architectural styles, all now in the care of the National Trust. For those walking by, perhaps the most impressive feature is the processional avenue of holm oak leading up to the manor.

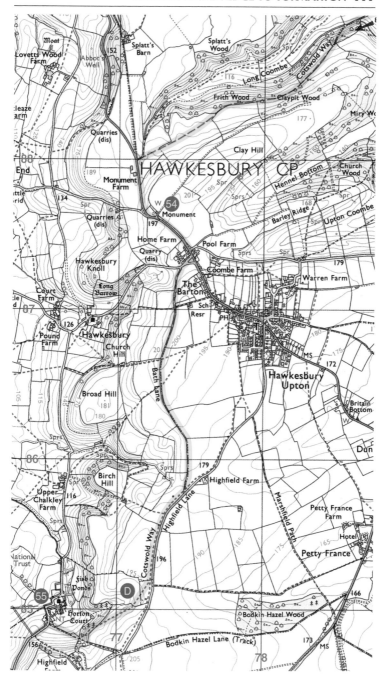

Horton Court, probably the oldest house passed along the Way. It has a Norman hall at its centre.

Turn left at the road. The small pond opposite contains a very large duck population. The view to the right is quite remarkable; fields of all shapes and sizes are divided from one another by hedges. Some of the odd shapes are dictated by natural features such as streams, but the rest seem merely arbitrary and represent boundaries first agreed many centuries ago. To the left the promontory has its almost obligatory hill-fort. The road reaches Horton by the village school. Turn right and immediately left onto a track that continues as a path between hedges leading to a stile, and then runs beside a wire fence. Where the fence turns off to the left, continue straight on to the wooden post in the field. The valley now drops steeply away towards a small reservoir. Beyond the reservoir take the obvious line across the field via stiles to the road. Turn right onto the road and left by Little Sodbury church **56**, which was rebuilt in 1859 on the site of the church that was William Tyndale's inspiration. The curious humps in the surrounding fields are pillow mounds, built up in medieval times as a rabbit warren to provide meat

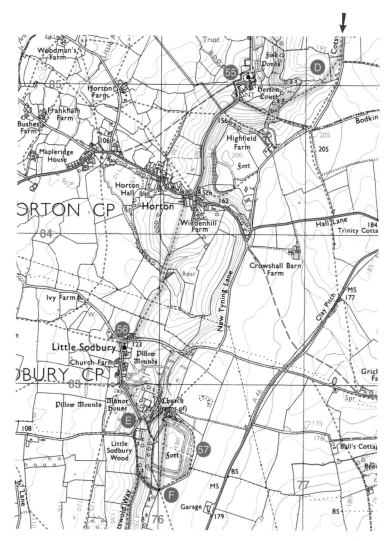

for the manor. At the top of the little hill, cross the road junction **E**, turn right up the footpath by the manor and then left through the iron gate. Climb the hill and turn right to go through the ditch and ramparts of the hill-fort **57**. The path crosses the plateau through the centre of the fort.

Leave the fort and head for the conifers **F**. Turn right, going downhill, and then left at the bottom to take the path beside the hedge. Beyond the farm **G**, cross the stile and join the lane. Turn right past the church **58**. Go through the churchyard and leave it by the kissing gate. There is a sad little memorial by the gate to a boy who died aged eleven; his tombstone is carved with his favourite animals, a pig and a mouse. Head diagonally across the next field to a gate in the hedge, then make for the stile to the left of the farm buildings and go down to the main road. Cross straight over and continue along Chapel Lane opposite. Where the cottages are set back from the road in a parking area, turn left through an iron gate **H** and take the path across the fields. At the next stile head for the post. A little ridge is now reached, giving good views across a gently undulating farming landscape. Turn right at the road. Just beyond the road junction, turn left to take the path across the fields to the driveway of Dodington Park.

The path now enters parkland **59**. It is important to keep to the recognised path through this private park, and the route is clearly waymarked by white posts. Cross the ornamental bridge and climb up the hill. At the top of the hill, the path goes round the woodland on the left. This is very typical parkland with carefully arranged clumps of trees, creating an idealised, romantic landscape. The route is easy to follow, and leads towards the far left-hand side of the line of trees on the horizon **I**.

Cross the road by the old milestone and continue on the same line over the next two roads. Cross the field and, at the roadway, turn left, then immediately right over another field that lurches downhill to the left. Head towards Tormarton church **60**. Turn right at the road, which continues to bend to the right, and then turn left by the Portcullis Inn. Go left again to leave the village by the track across the fields.

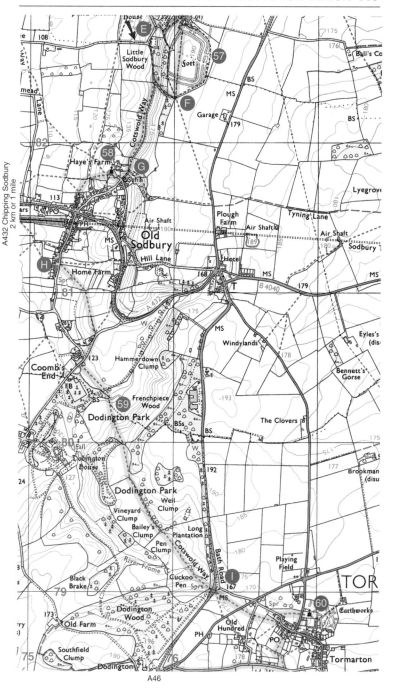

7 TORMARTON TO BATH

via Cold Ashton

Leaving Tormarton, cross the field to the stone stile and take the path to the left. The blue motorway sign comes into view, though the noise of the motorway has been present for some time. At the road turn right past a row of cottages with ogee arched windows. A rather grander house follows and the road advances towards a charming little rotunda beyond an impressive gateway. Turn left at the road junction **A** and left again to walk alongside the very busy A46 to the motorway roundabout. Take the left-hand side of the interchange across the M4 to continue down the A46. Cross to the far side of the carriageway to follow the path beside the road to the picnic area **B** beyond the council depot. Go across the car park, take the footpath to the left and continue along the edge of the wood, where there are good views across the Severn to the hills of Wales. Follow the path beside the hedge, and turn left at the gateway to continue on the

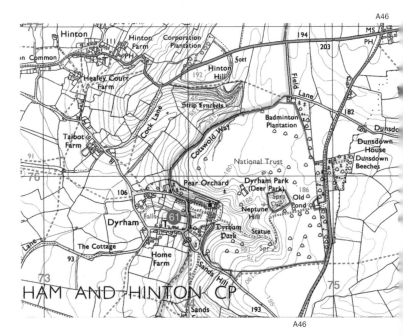

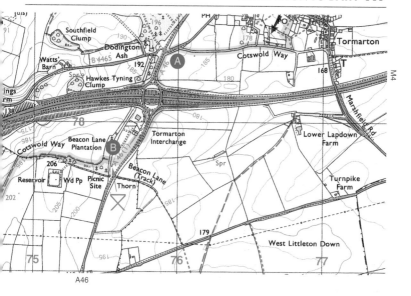

path by the field through a very open landscape. The noise of cars is now replaced by the sweet song of the yellowhammers, which are later joined by skylarks.

At the end of the fields, cross the road and continue on the minor road immediately opposite. Where this turns sharply left, turn right to follow the path beside the wall that surrounds Dyrham Park. The path comes out on the edge of the escarpment, which is altogether gentler than it was further north, with softly moulded valleys. Continue on the grassy path beside the wall; an impressive set of strip lynchets comes into view on the opposite side of the little valley. Over in the distance, the tower blocks of Bristol can be seen. Continue following the wall as it swings round to the left by the metal gate and, at the next gate, head downhill along the sunken lane. At the road turn left to pass the ornamental gates of Dyrham Park **61**. A magnificent sweep of lawn leads to an equally splendid house, built between 1691 and 1710. Its prominent balustrade, terrace and double staircase show the influence of its French architect, yet it sits very easily in an English landscape. Unfortunately there is no access from the walk as the entrance is round the far side on the A46. It is, however, possible to visit the medieval church tucked away beside the house.

At the road junction turn left and, just beyond the houses on the right, turn right over the stile to follow the path beside the hedge. This goes gently downhill past a couple of ponds which are comparatively

Deer graze outside Dyrham Park, built in the French style at the end of the seventeenth century.

new creations. The route now leads across the middle of one field, then along the edge of the next, towards Dyrham Wood. Where the wire fence goes round to the left, continue straight across the field, heading for the left-hand side of the long line of trees **C**. Cross the little stream and climb the steps up to the stile. The official route heads off at a slight diagonal, but it is probably easier to go round the edge to the left. Cross the stile to take the narrow path through an old hazel coppice, now somewhat neglected. Leaving the wood, follow the path along the side of the hedge, then follow the stone wall round to the right by the farm buildings and go down to the road. Turn left onto the road, then right onto the footpath by the hedge to arrive at the busy A46(T). Make a beeline for the stile opposite and take the path that runs diagonally to the left across the field to a stone stile in the corner, then continue to bear left across the next field, heading for the house. Turn left at the main road (the A420). Opposite the White Hart **D**, turn right to cross the road and take the track down to the church **62**. This is an unassuming building with one grand and elaborate feature, a canopied pulpit of the early sixteenth century. Leaving the church, go down to the road and turn right into Cold Ashton. This is also the starting point for the circular walk on p. 130.

Cold Ashton sits on the rim of the valley, from where it has magnificent views. There are two grand houses, the old rectory, which hides behind a stone wall and ornamental entrance, and the manor house.

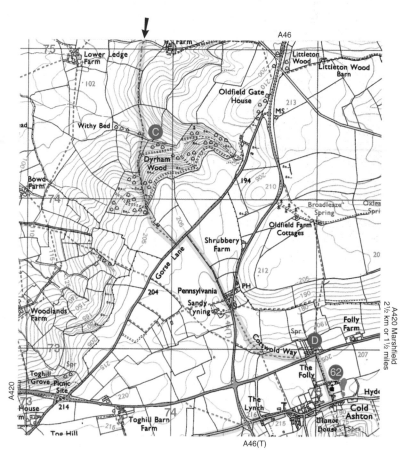

The imposing manor house at Cold Ashton stands on the rim of a hill and enjoys

nagnificent views.

The Civil War earthworks on Lansdown Hill, from which the Royalists under Sir Bevil Grenville attacked the Parliamentarians.

Continue straight on at the road junction and cross over the A46 onto the green way opposite, bordered by a drystone wall on one side and a hedge on the other. This is a landscape of gentle curves, where even field boundaries seldom run in straight lines. The hills, however, are steep enough to have caused the medieval farmers to turn to strip lynchets for cultivation. At the bottom of the hill, where the track runs round to the left, carry straight on down the path that crosses a tiny stream **E**. Continue across the field, keeping the large pond on the left, and follow the same line across the next field. Go through the gate to the right of the barn. Turn left at the broad track, cross the cattle grid and at the next cattle grid turn right to walk on a diagonal up the steep hillside. At the top of the hill is a bench, offering a chance to sit back and enjoy as good a view as any to be had on the walk **63**.

At the brow of the hill, cross the stile and turn right towards the next stile, then right again at the lane. The Grenville Monument now comes into view. The Way curves round the top of the hill on a stony path bordered by hedges. A feature of this part of the walk is the way in which each hilltop offers not just a different view, but an altogether different type of view. The fields and houses seen from the last bench seemed almost intimate; now it is the distant prospect that demands attention. Closer at hand are outcrops of exposed stone. As the path winds uphill, turn off just before the crest to cross the stile in the stone wall. Follow the path alongside the wall and on into the little wood, which includes a number of elm trees that have survived the ravages of disease.

The path emerges at a monument commemorating Sir Bevil Grenville **64**, who died in the Civil War battle fought here. The Parliamentarian forces had formed up on Lansdown Hill, from where they launched a series of attacks on the Royalists down in the valley. Sir Bevil led the charge that drove the Parliamentarians off the hill, but died in the action. From the monument, follow the path to the main road.

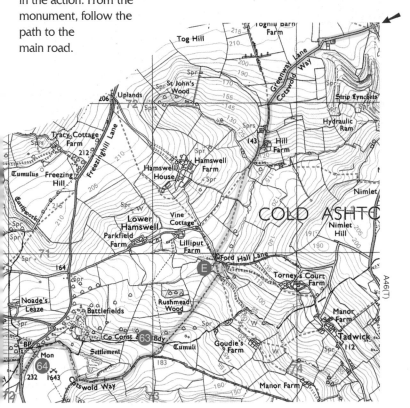

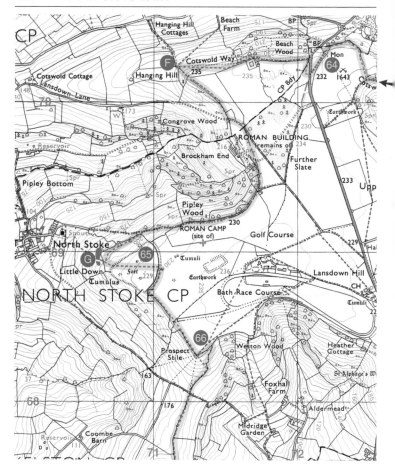

Cross the road and turn right onto the tarmacked path that runs parallel to the road, then left beside the wood. Just before the Fire Brigade communications tower, turn right to leave the roadway on a footpath. Go through the hunting gate, and a wide vista appears with Bristol at the centre. Before the little wood is reached **F**, cross a stile near the trig point to take the path round the rim of the valley, leading onto the golf course. Keep to the wall along the edge of the wood. At the end of the wood, turn right across the golf course and continue on the track between this and the trees that grow up the hillside.

Where the woodland ends, turn away from the golf course onto the path that runs through the rough grass of the hillside. Leave the broad track by the fallen tree to take the grassy path up to the iron gate on the left. Up the hill are the ramparts of the promontory fort **65**, the last of the Iron Age forts to be met on the walk. On reaching a wooden post **G**, the Cotswold Way turns left; the path to the right is the start of the North Stoke circular walk (see p. 132). The River Avon can be seen down below. At the top of the promontory, aim for the gap in the bank opposite. Once through this gap, one can see the bank and ditch that were the defences of the fort. Turn right along the ramparts, then left along the edge of the hill, passing the end of Bath racecourse. At the corner of the plateau is a topograph **66** and the aptly named Prospect Stile, with a view which for the first time includes the city of Bath.

Cross the stile, turn left through the gate, then right and right again on a dogleg, and carry on towards the hill with a crown of trees. This is a narrow bridleway running between a hedge and a wire fence. Some of the muddier sections are paralleled by a separate footpath and eventually it all opens out onto a road. Go straight ahead and, where the road turns off to the left, carry on across the stile to take the path that follows the contour round the brow of the hill. The first identifiable feature in Georgian Bath is, perversely, the Victorian gasworks. From the trig point **67** a grassy path leads down to the houses. Cross the stile and go downhill to the sports field.

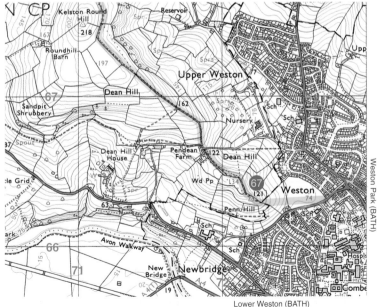

Lower Weston (BATH)

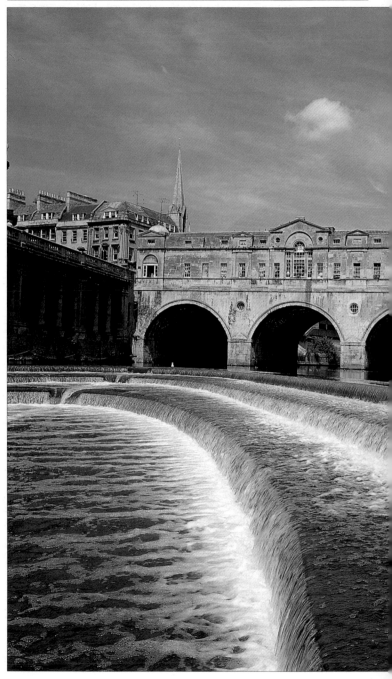

The weir across the Avon at Bath. Behind the classical façade of Pulteney Bridge

nventional row of shops.

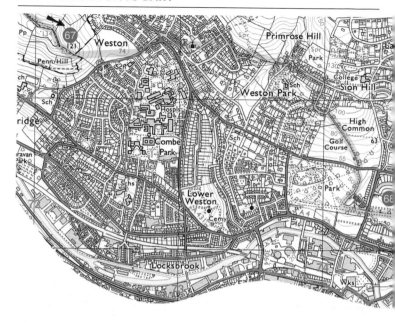

The route through Bath can hardly be said to begin by presenting the famous city at its best. This is a suburban stroll which, with seeming perversity, takes the walker who has just come downhill to the city edge, back uphill again to its northern fringes. There is, however, method in this apparent madness, for the final section reveals Bath at its grandest. Take the path across the playing field to the gate in the corner and turn left into Penn Hill Road, going straight on down Anchor Road. Turn left at the bottom of this road, then go over the pedestrian crossing, turn right and walk along Church Street on the high-level pavement. Go through the churchyard, round the church and left into Church Road. Continue up a little alleyway and turn right at the top of the road. Turn left up the dead-end road and, at the top, turn left into an alleyway, crossing a stile to take the stony path down to a kissing gate. Go up a very steep lane, and follow the continuation of the same lane to come out at Summerhill Road, which has a line of trees down the centre. At the end, turn right down Sion Hill, and Bath at last begins to appear in a more elegant guise.

Turn right again to take the path across High Common, with a view of the first of many Georgian terraces over to the left. Continue on to Victoria Park and the Victoria Monument, turning left along Royal Avenue. Over to the left is Royal Crescent **68**, designed by

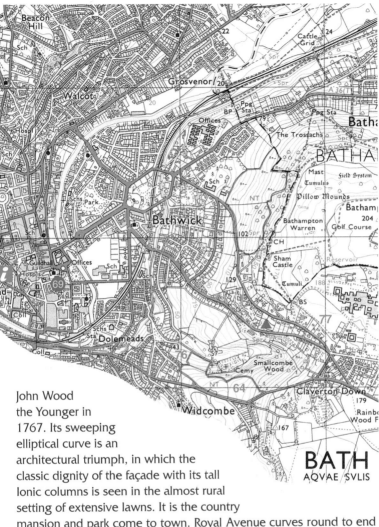

John Wood the Younger in 1767. Its sweeping elliptical curve is an architectural triumph, in which the classic dignity of the façade with its tall Ionic columns is seen in the almost rural setting of extensive lawns. It is the country mansion and park come to town. Royal Avenue curves round to end in Queen Square. The end of the walk is now close by, and the official route follows a succession of short streets – Wood Street, Quiet Street, New Bond Street, New Bond Street Place and Union Passage – to arrive at Bath Abbey **69**.

To describe the pleasures of Bath would demand far more space than this book can supply, and is not even necessary. This is a city where delights are constantly to be found, from the Roman baths to Pulteney Bridge, Bath's version of the Ponte Vecchio of Florence. No country walk could ask for a grander finale.

CIRCULAR WALK FROM COLD ASHTON

4¹/₂ miles (7 km)

The walk starts at the point **A** where the Cotswold Way comes into Cold Ashton from the north past the church **62**. Instead of turning right to follow the Way, turn left up the road. Ignore the first Public Footpath sign. The road now rises very gently uphill with a view over the Wiltshire Downs to the east. At the second footpath sign, turn right through the gap in the hedge and head downhill towards the corner of the field, where it narrows towards an iron gate. The path now continues downhill along a deep hollow and swings round to the left along the shoulder of the hill. This is a delightful valley which seems quite cut off from the rest of the world.

The route heads up the valley, through the obvious gap in the hedge. A small stream, its line marked by trees, wanders along the valley floor. The path and stream gradually converge. As one approaches the head of the valley, the sides begin to close in and the tall trees give way to more modest scrub. Where the way is barred by a wire fence **B**, go uphill to the right, cross the stile and turn right up the green lane. The trees on either side form a canopy overhead, and a landscape of large fields, consisting of mixed arable and pasture, can be seen through breaks in the cover.

At the road, turn left, then right onto the bridleway by the stone pillar. The wayside flowers attract a variety of butterflies. Where the bridleway goes through an S-bend, turn right across the stile by the iron gate and follow the path at the top of the hill, round by the fence. A splendid view opens out over a procession of hills and valleys, accompanied by the clear, pure song of the lark. The trudge down the bridleway is here replaced by a springy walk over turf, above the deep, wooded valley. At the stile **C** the old footpath has been rerouted and the new path is waymarked by yellow arrows. Turn left to follow the line of the hedgerow and continue on round the field at the rim of the valley. Another hidden green valley comes into view, this time a little broader and not quite so steep-sided. Continue on to a lane. Cross straight over on two stiles, then follow the hedge round to the right, leaving the field by the stile and heading straight off downhill **D**. The next stile can be seen in the right-hand corner of the field; it leads directly to a footbridge over a

130

stream. The route continues straight on, following the line of the stream; the deviation has now ended.

The path passes below a stone cottage, known as Beek's Mill. Although the house still stands, little of the mill itself remains apart from the leat **70**. Cross over the stream and head straight up the small hill crowned with trees. Cross the stile by the wooden gate and turn right onto the road. The road winds uphill between trees and grassy banks on which speedwell, cow parsley and greater stitchwort are in evidence. At Fry's Farm, turn right onto the broad track between the house and the barns. As the path gradually climbs the hill, so Cold Ashton comes into view, lined up along the ridge. On reaching a grassy field, head for the gate by the prominent tree. Turn right immediately before the stile, onto the path beside the hedge. Turn right at the road to Cold Ashton. At the road junction turn right again to return to the start.

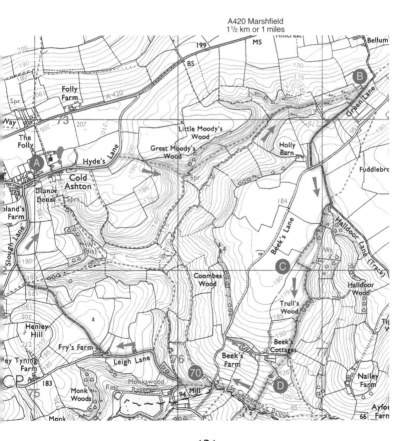

CIRCULAR WALK: NORTH STOKE AND THE AVON VALLEY

5 miles (8 km)

Leave the Cotswold Way at Little Down hill-fort **65**, following the path downhill to North Stoke church with its memorial to churchwarden William Britten. The little stream that runs by the churchyard dashes through a series of small falls before disappearing underground. Join the road that leads down to the village, starting at a raised, cobbled pavement. It is bordered by handsome stone houses, a number of which have sophisticated details. Where the road divides, just beyond the telephone box, turn right **A**.

The road soon begins to go steeply downhill, giving a fine view across the Avon valley. The river snakes through the landscape and, over to the left, a line of white foam stretching almost the full width of the river marks the position of the weir. Alongside, by the bank, is the artificial cutting containing the lock to raise and lower boats. At the foot of the hill turn right beside the main road and, after a few yards, cross over to join the path by the Public Footpath sign. Enter the field and turn left to follow the riverside Avon Walkway. The path leads to a stile; once in the next field, head towards the gap between the buildings. Over to the right are two truncated stone pyramids – all that remain of the Kelston brass mills **71**, established here in the 1760s. Brass hardens quickly when being worked, and these annealing furnaces were used to keep it malleable. The path runs behind a row of cottages, built for the millworkers.

Beyond the cottages, follow the path through the metal gate, down to the riverbank immediately above the weir. Cross the stile just before the railway bridge and turn left up the embankment. The disused railway line **B** was built in 1869 by the Midland Railway to compete with the Great Western route from London to Bristol. It was closed in 1966 and has found a new use as a cycle path and walkway between Bath and Bristol.

Turn right onto the old line. At the site of the old Saltford station, a wooden owl looks out, appropriately enough, at the Bird in Hand pub. The path goes through a deep cutting crossed by a high-arched bridge of blue engineering brick on stone abutments. There is more sculpture along the way – intertwined figures in wood, followed by an array of carved stones. Go over the second river bridge and take the path down the embankment to the right, then cross the stile and continue on along the riverbank towards the glasshouses.

The path follows the river as it swings in gentle, sweeping curves between grassy banks. To the left is the tower of Bitton church. Just before the huddle of buildings at Swineford, a small watercourse appears, running into the river. This is the outflow from Swineford Mill **72**, established in 1840 for working copper. The path follows the line of the watercourse, and one can still see the arches under the building through which the water flowed to turn a pair of wheels. Cross the stile opposite the Swan public house. Cross the road, turn right and then left to take the path through the gap between the farm and the cottages towards a picnic site **C**. Beyond the farm buildings, an artificial watercourse runs downhill in an attractive waterfall; it was originally built to power a small iron foundry that once stood here. Turn right at the watercourse in the direction indicated by the yellow arrows. Cross the stile and head for another stile opposite, following the waymarked path across the fields and up the hill. At the top of the fields, the path becomes a narrow tree-shaded lane, still climbing steeply uphill, its banks smothered in lesser celandine. It eventually emerges in the village.

Turn left at the road to retrace the route back to the start.

133

The Royal Crescent, Bath, a superb example of Georgian architecture in this mos

elegant of cities.

USEFUL
INFORMATION

TRANSPORT

Getting to the Cotswold Way

Train services run from London to Bath, Stroud and Cheltenham, Moreton-in-Marsh and Evesham. Stratford-upon-Avon can be reached from Birmingham.

Chipping Campden can be reached by bus from Stratford-upon-Avon, Moreton-in-Marsh and Evesham. Express coaches connect to Bath, Cheltenham and Broadway.

Information about road services can be obtained from Public Transport Officers at the following County Councils:

Hereford & Worcester County Hall, Spetchley Road, Worcester WR5 2NP (tel. 01905 763763)
Gloucestershire Shire Hall, Gloucester GL1 2TG (tel. 01452 425543)
Avon Avon House, Haymarket, Bristol BS99 7DE (tel. 0117 929 0777)

Information regarding coach operators and services, taxis and private car hire is contained in *The Cotswold Way Handbook*, obtainable from the Ramblers' Association at the address on p. 140.

ACCOMMODATION

The Cotswold Way Handbook (see *Transport*) gives detailed information on accommodation on the Cotswold Way, including camping facilities. Other bed and breakfast accommodation is given in guides such as *The Good Bed and Breakfast Guide*.

There are two youth hostels on the Cotswold Way at:

GR 983267   Rock House, Cleeve Hill, Cheltenham, Glos GL52 3PR (tel. 01242 672065)

GR 766644   Bathwick Hill, Bath BA2 6JZ (tel. 01225 465674)

TOURIST INFORMATION CENTRES

Heart of England Tourist Board Larkhill Road, Worcester WR5 2EF (tel. 01905 763436)

West Country Tourist Board 60 St David's Hill, Exeter EX4 4SY (tel. 01392 76351)

Bath The Colonnades, 11–13 Bath Street, Bath BA1 1SW (tel. 01225 462831)

Broadway 1 Cotswold Court, The Green, Broadway, Worcs WR12 7AA (tel. 01386 852937)

Cheltenham 77 Promenade, Cheltenham, Glos GL50 1PP (tel. 01242 522878)

Chipping Campden Woolstaplers' Hall Museum, High Street, Chipping Campden, Glos GL55 6HB (tel. 01386 840101)

Painswick The Library, Stroud Road, Painswick, Glos GL6 6DT (tel. 01452 813552)

Stroud Subscription Rooms, George Street, Stroud, Glos GL5 1AE (tel. 01453 765768)

Winchcombe The Town Hall, High Street, Winchcombe, Glos GL54 5LJ (tel. 01242 602925)

USEFUL ADDRESSES

British Trust for Ornithology, Beech Grove, Tring, Herts HP12 5NR

Cotswold Countryside Service, County Planning Dept, Shire Hall, Gloucester GL1 2TN (tel. 01452 425674)

The Countryside Commission, John Dower House, Crescent Place, Cheltenham, Glos GL50 3RA (tel. 01242 521381)

English Heritage (South West Region), 7–8 King Street, Bristol BS1 4EQ (tel. 0117 975 0700)

English Nature

Head Office: Northminster House, Peterborough PE1 1UA (tel. 01733 340345)

Somerset & Avon: Roughmoor, Bishops Hull, Taunton, Somerset TA1 5AA (tel. 01823 283211)

The Three Counties Team, Masefield House, Wells Road, Malvern Wells, Worcs WR14 4PA (tel. 01684 560616)

The National Trust

Head Office: 36 Queen Anne's Gate, London SW1H 9AS (tel. 0171 222 9251)

Severn Region: Mythe End House, Tewkesbury, Glos GL20 6EB (tel. 01684 850051)

Wessex Region: Eastleigh Court, Bishopstow, Warminster, Wilts
BA12 9HW (tel. 01985 847777)

Ordnance Survey, Romsey Road, Maybush, Southampton SO16 4GU

Ramblers' Association, 1–5 Wandsworth Road, London SW8 2XX
(tel. 0171 582 6878)

Royal Society for Nature Conservation, The Green, Witham Park,
Waterside South, Lincoln LN5 7JR (tel. 01522 544400)

Royal Society for the Protection of Birds, The Lodge, Sandy, Beds
SG19 2DL

Wildlife Trusts

Bristol, Bath & Avon: The Wildlife Centre, 32 Jacobs Wells Road,
Bristol BS8 1DR (tel. 0117 926 8018)

Gloucestershire: Gloucestershire Trust for Nature Conservation,
Dulverton Building, Robinswood Hill Country Park, Reservoir
Road, Gloucester GL4 9SX (tel. 01452 383333)

Worcestershire: The Worcestershire Nature Conservation Trust,
Lower Smite Farm, Smite Hill, Hindlip, Worcs WR3 8SZ
(tel. 01905 754919)

Youth Hostels Association, Trevelyan House, 8 St Stephens Hill, St
Albans, Herts AL1 2DY (tel. 01727 55215)

Ordnance Survey maps covering the Cotswold Way

Landranger Maps
(scale 1:50 000)
150 Worcester and the
  Malverns
151 Stratford-upon-Avon
162 Gloucester and the
  Forest of Dean
163 Cheltenham and
  Cirencester
172 Bristol and Bath

Pathfinder Maps (scale 1:25 000)
1043 Broadway and Chipping
  Campden
1066 Cheltenham
1067 Winchcombe and Stow-on-the-
  Wold
1089 Gloucester
1113 Stroud
1132 Dursley and Wotton-under-
  Edge
1133 Nailsworth and Tetbury
1151 Patchway and Chipping Sodbury
1167 Bristol East
1183 Bath and Keynsham
Touring Map
8 The Cotswolds (shows only part of
  the route)

BIBLIOGRAPHY

Barraclough, Marian, *Exploring The Cotswold Edge*, Thornhill Press, 1979

Bloemendal, F., & Hollingsworth, A., *Cotswold Architecture & Heritage*, Ian Allan, 1992

— *Cotswold Landscape*, Ian Allan, 1991

Birch, Sally and Hill, Michael, *Cotswold Stone Houses*, Alan Sutton, 1994

Brill, Edith, *Life and Tradition on the Cotswolds*, Alan Sutton, 1990

— *Cotswold Crafts*, Batsford, 1977

Crosher, G.R., *Along the Cotswold Ways*, Cassell, 1976

Cunliffe, Barry, *The City of Bath*, Alan Sutton, 1986

Derrick, Freda, *Cotswold Stone*, Chapman and Hall, 1948

Dixon, Reginald, *Cotswold Curiosities*, The Dovecote Press, 1988

Donaldson, D.N., *A Portrait of Winchcombe*, published by the author, 1978

Dyer, James, *The Cotswolds and the Upper Thames*, Shire Publications, 1970

Finberg, H.P.R., *The Gloucestershire Landscape*, Hodder & Stoughton, 1975

Gordon, C., *Chipping Campden*, Alan Sutton, 1994

Greensted, M., *The Arts and Crafts Movement in the Cotswolds*, Alan Sutton, 1993

Hadfield, Charles and Alice Mary, *The Cotswolds*, Batsford, 1966

— *Introducing the Cotswolds*, David & Charles, 1976

— *The Cotswolds: A New Study*, David & Charles, 1976

Houghton, C.C., *A Walk about Broadway*, Ian Allan, 1980

Hyett, F.A., *Glimpses of the History of Painswick*, British Publishing Co., 1957

Lindley, E.S., *Wotton-under-Edge*, Museum Press, 1962

McWhirr, A., *Roman Gloucestershire*, Alan Sutton, 1986

Mills, Stephen and Riemer, Pierce, *The Mills of Gloucestershire*, Quotes Limited, 1989

Morris, R.K., and Hoverd, K., *The Buildings of Bath*, Alan Sutton, 1993

Ordnance Survey Landranger Guidebook to the Cotswolds, Jarrold, 1989

Powell, Geoffrey, *The Book of Campden*, Quotes Limited, 1982

Ramblers' Association, Gloucestershire Area, *The Cotswold Way Handbook*, published annually

Robertson, Charles, *Bath: An Architectural Guide*, Faber, 1975
Smith, Brian S., *The Cotswolds*, Alan Sutton, 1992
Tann, Jennifer, *Gloucestershire Woollen Mills*, David & Charles, 1967
Verey, David, *Cotswold Churches*, Alan Sutton, 1991
— *Buildings of England: Gloucestershire* (vol 1: *The Cotswolds*),
    Penguin Books, 1970
Wright, Louise and Priddey, James, *Cotswold Heritage*, Hale, 1979

Places to visit on or near the Cotswold Way

Woolstaplers' Hall Museum, High Street, Chipping Campden
Broadway Tower Country Park
Snowshill Manor
Gloucestershire and Warwickshire Steam Railway, Toddington Station
Stanway House
Hailes Abbey
Winchcombe Folk Museum, Town Hall, Winchcombe
Winchcombe Railway Museum, 23 Gloucester Street
Winchcombe Pottery
Wadfield Roman Villa
Sudeley Castle and Gardens
Cheltenham Art Gallery and Museum, Clarence Street, Cheltenham
Gustav Holst Birthplace Museum, 4 Clarence Road, Pittville,
    Cheltenham
Pittville Pump Room and Museum, Pittville Park, Cheltenham
Crickley Windward Vineyard and Winery, Green Lane, Little
    Witcombe
Crickley Hill Country Park
Great Witcombe Roman Villa
Cooper's Hill Local Nature Reserve
Prinknash Abbey
Prinknash Pottery
Prinknash Bird Park
Painswick Rococo Garden, The Stables, Painswick House
Rooksmoor Mills, Bath Road, Stroud
Stroud District Museum, Lansdown, Stroud
Stroud Subscription Rooms, George Street, Stroud
Woodchester Park Mansion, Nympsfield
Frocester Court Tithe Barn
Hetty Pegler's Tump, Nympsfield

Owlpen Manor, Uley
Tyndale Monument
Newark Park
Kingswood Abbey Gatehouse
Hawkesbury Monument
Horton Court
Dyrham Park
Avon Valley Railway, Bitton Station
Beckfords Tower, Lansdown Road
Sir Bevil Grenville's Monument, Lansdown
Bath
   Postal Museum, 8 Broad Street
   Book Museum, Manvers Street
   Mr Bowler's Business, Bath Industrial Heritage Centre, Camden
      Works, Julian Road
   The Building of Bath Museum, Countess of Huntingdon's Chapel,
      The Vineyards, The Paragon
   Georgian Garden, Gravel Walk
   Guildhall, High Street
   Holburne Museum and Crafts Study Centre, Great Pulteney Street
   Sally Lunn's House, 4 North Parade Passage
   Museum of Costume, Assembly Rooms, Bennett Street
   The Museum of East Asian Art, 12 Bennett Street
   Museum of English Naive Art
   Roman Baths Museum, Abbey Church Yard
   No. 1 Royal Crescent
   The Royal Photographic Society, Milsom Street
   Victoria Art Gallery, Bridge Street